*The Journal of Andrew Fuller Studies*

Published in the United States of America by
by The Andrew Fuller Center for Baptist Studies
The Southern Baptist Theological Seminary
2825 Lexington Road
Louisville, Kentucky 40280

© The Andrew Fuller Center for Baptist Studies 2022

All rights reserved. No part of this publication may be reproduced, stored in a retrieval system, or transmitted, in any form or by any means, without the prior permission in writing of The Andrew Fuller Center for Baptist Studies, or as expressly permitted by law, by license, or under terms agreed with the appropriate reproduction rights organization.

ISBN 978-1-77484-084-9

Printed by H&E Publishing, Peterborough, Ontario, Canada

# *The Journal of Andrew Fuller Studies*

---

The *Journal of Andrew Fuller Studies* is an open access, double-blind peer-reviewed, scholarly journal published online biannually in February and September by the Andrew Fuller Center for Baptist Studies (under the auspices of The Southern Baptist Theological Seminary). The publication language of the journal is English. Articles that deal with the life, ministry, and thought of the Baptist pastor-theologian Andrew Fuller are very welcome, as well as essays on his friends, his Particular Baptist community in the long eighteenth century (1680s–1830s), and the global impact of his thought, known as "Fullerism."

Articles and book reviews are to follow generally the style of Kate L. Turabian, *A Manual for Writers of Research Papers, Theses, and Dissertations*, 9$^{th}$ ed. (Chicago: University of Chicago Press, 2018). They may be submitted in British, American, Australian, New Zealand, or Canadian English. Articles should be between 5,000 and 8,000 words, excluding footnotes. Articles are to be sent to the Editor and book reviews to the Book Review Editors.

*Editor*:
Michael A G Haykin, ThD, FRHistS
Chair & Professor of Church History
& Director, The Andrew Fuller Center for Baptist Studies
The Southern Baptist Theological Seminary, Louisville, Kentucky
mhaykin@sbts.edu

*Associate editors*:
Baiyu Andrew Song, PhD cand.
Assistant Professor of General Education Studies
Heritage College and Seminary
Cambridge, Ontario
bsong@heritagecs.edu

Chance Faulkner, MTh cand.
Director, Union Publishing, Wales
director@unionpublishing.org

*Design editor*:
Dustin W. Benge, PhD
Associate Professor of Biblical Spirituality and Historical Theology
& Vice President of Communications
The Southern Baptist Theological Seminary, Louisville, Kentucky

*Book review editor*:
C. Anthony Neel, PhD cand.
The Southern Baptist Theological Seminary, Louisville, Kentucky
cneel914@students.sbts.edu

*Editorial board:*
Cindy Aalders, DPhil
Director of the John Richard Allison Library
& Assistant Professor of the History of Christianity
Regent College, Vancouver

Dustin Benge, PhD
Associate Professor of Biblical Spirituality and Historical Theology
& Vice President of Communications
The Southern Baptist Theological Seminary
Louisville, Kentucky

Dustin B. Bruce, PhD
Dean & Assistant Professor of Christian Theology and Church History
Boyce College
Louisville, Kentucky

Ian Hugh Clary, PhD
Assistant Professor of Historical Theology
Colorado Christian University, Lakewood, Colorado
iclary@ccu.edu

Chris W. Crocker, PhD
Pastor, Markdale Baptist Church, ON
& Associate Professor of Church History
Toronto Baptist Seminary
Toronto, Ontario

Chris Chun, PhD
Professor of Church History & Director of the Jonathan Edwards Center
Gateway Seminary
Ontario, California

Jenny-Lyn de Klerk, PhD
Editor, Book Division
Crossway
Wheaton, Illinois

Jason G. Duesing, PhD
Provost & Professor of Historical Theology
Midwestern Baptist Theological Seminary
Kansas City, Missouri

Nathan A. Finn, PhD
Provost & Dean of the University Faculty
North Greenville University
Tigerville, South Carolina

C. Ryan Griffith, PhD
Pastor, Cities Church
St. Paul, Minnesota

Peter J. Morden, PhD
Senior Pastor/Team Leader, Cornerstone Baptist Church
Leeds, England
& Distinguished Visiting Scholar
Spurgeon's College
London, England

Adriaan C. Neele, PhD
Director, Doctoral Program & Professor of Historical Theology
Puritan Reformed Theological Seminary
Grand Rapids, Michigan
& Research Scholar
Yale University, Jonathan Edwards Center
New Haven, Connecticut

Robert Strivens, PhD
Pastor, Bradford on Avon Baptist Church (UK)
& Lecturer in Church History
London Seminary
London, England

Tom Nettles, PhD
Senior Professor of Historical Theology
The Southern Baptist Theological Seminary
Louisville, Kentucky

Blair Waddell, PhD
Pastor, Providence Baptist Church
Huntsville, Alabama

# Contents

*The Journal of Andrew Fuller Studies*
No. 5, September 2022

| | |
|---|---:|
| **Editorial**<br>Michael A.G. Haykin | 9 |
| **Articles** | |
| "The soul's joy in God as its portion:"<br>Particular Baptist piety and poverty from the<br>English Civil War to the Industrial Revolution<br>*Nathan Tarr* | 11 |
| A bibliography of the writings of John Collett Ryland<br>*Garrett M. Walden* | 33 |
| "To promote the love of Christ:" Joseph Priestley, Andrew Fuller,<br>and the deity of Christ as the basis for Christian morality<br>*Andrew B. Lawson* | 49 |
| In the midst of his afflictions:<br>Andrew Fuller as suffering missionary-theologian of the Spirit<br>*Nicholas J. Abraham* | 61 |
| Biblical meditation in the life of Andrew Fuller<br>*Ronald C. Barnes* | 73 |
| **Texts & documents** | |
| Three prayers from John Collett Ryland,<br>*Introduction to the Knowledge of the Holy Spirit*<br>ed. *Garrett M. Walden and Michael A.G. Haykin* | 101 |
| James Hinton on the assurance of the Father's love<br>ed. *Chance Faulkner* | 105 |
| "Of the future happiness of infants I have no doubt:"<br>James Hinton on the death of a child<br>ed. *Chance Faulkner* | 109 |
| Joseph Kinghorn's pedagogical advice to William Newman<br>ed. *Baiyu Andrew Song* | 113 |
| **Book reviews** | 127 |

# Editorial

Michael A.G. Haykin

Michael A.G. Haykin is Chair and Professor of Church History and Director, The Andrew Fuller Center for Baptist Studies at The Southern Baptist Theological Seminary, Louisville, Kentucky.

---

Being a doctoral supervisor of students at The Southern Baptist Theological Seminary, and one or two other schools, has been a tremendous experience. Not only has it brought me into contact with very fine younger Christian scholars whose scholarship, I trust, will enrich the Church Militant in the years to come, but many of them have become fast and dear friends. You cannot walk together with such men and women for five or six years (the normal time for a PhD at Southern) and not build into one another's lives. Inevitably, then, there is a pastoral component to doctoral supervision.

Recently, one of my doctoral students experienced a harrowing tragedy: he and his dear wife lost their youngest child, their only daughter among five children, to a drowning accident. When he called me to tell me of this tragedy, I sat and listened to his sorrow and wept with him. Later, while preparing this edition of *The Journal of Andrew Fuller Studies*, I re-read the letter that James Hinton of Oxford wrote to a grieving parent, who had also lost an infant child. His words then are a deep comfort now: "They [children] die because Adam sinned; they live because Jesus died." This is an academic journal with all of the rigour that one would expect of such, but we can never forget that the material we deal with is also the stuff of pastoral life, for Andrew Fuller and the men and women who feature in these pages were first and foremost deeply involved in the lives of local churches.

In this issue we also are pleased to have a number of academic essays: first, a thematic study of Particular Baptist thought about poverty and piety by Nathan

Tarr, the newly-appointed Associate Professor of Pastoral Theology and Director of the DMin program at Phoenix Seminary; then, the first complete listing of the works of John Collett Ryland, an author with a voluminous pen, which has been compiled by Southern Seminary doctoral student Garrett M. Walden; third, an essay on Andrew Fuller's linking the deity of the Christ to Christian virtue in his response to Socinianism by Andrew B. Lawson, also a Southern doctoral student; fourth, a study of Fuller's experience of suffering as the setting for his theological reflections by Nicholas J. Abraham, yet another doctoral student at Southern; and finally, an essay on Andrew Fuller's practice and experience of meditation by Ronald Barnes, an Ontario pastor. This final essay is drawn from Barnes' DMin thesis, "Think on the Word: Biblical Meditation in the Life of Andrew Fuller (1754–1815) and the Tradition In Which He Stood" (The Southern Baptist Theological Seminary, 2019).

And we also have a few documents, including the Hinton letter mentioned above, which has been transcribed and introduced by Chance Faulkner, and some book reviews. I am deeply grateful to all who have made this issue of the journal possible, including my associate editor Baiyu Andrew Song, Dustin Benge, who did the layout and design, and Chance Faulkner, the journal's publisher.

# "The soul's joy in God as its portion:" Particular Baptist piety and poverty from the English Civil War to the Industrial Revolution

Nathan Tarr

Nathan Tarr (PhD, The Southern Baptist Theological Seminary), Associate Professor of Pastoral Theology; Director of Doctor of Ministry Program, Phoenix Seminary, Scottsdale, AZ

---

This article surveys three Particular Baptist responses to the issue of poverty between the English Civil Wars (1642–1651) and the beginning of the Industrial Revolution (1760–1840).[1] Specifically, it examines the manner in which John Bunyan (1628–1688), the Particular Baptist General Assembly (meeting annually from 1689–1692), and Anne Dutton (1692–1765) appropriated the biblical language of wealth and poverty in responding to the deprivation they saw around them in society, and many Baptists experienced first-hand. The claim in the article is not that these examples exhaust the variations but illustrate the common foundation of Particular Baptist attempts to bring their piety into alignment with the biblical perspective on wealth and poverty.

At its most basic, the Particular Baptist response insisted on (1) the goodness of temporal wealth rightly stewarded, (2) though believers should expect to feel want in this world, (3) a pang tempered by the spiritual riches often received through these very deprivations. It should be acknowledged from the beginning, however, that these three affirmations are ordered according to the ascending amount of emphasis they received in Particular Baptist thought. This means that the spiritual destitution introduced by sin and the over-towering riches of divine grace was the ultimate Particular Baptist application of

---

[1] The industrial revolution altered not only the expression of poverty but the scope of potential responses as well. To take a rather magnificent example of the latter, see the philanthropic work of the 19th century Baptist John D. Rockefeller (1839–1937).

scripture's financial vocabulary.

*Following the Reformers*
As with their piety and practice more generally, Particular Baptist responses to poverty largely followed the contours of their theological heritage. This pedigree included, most immediately, the Congregationalist Puritans; and before that, the approach forged by the Protestant reformers.[2] A full exploration of these antecedents is warranted but must be deferred here to existing treatments.[3] One aspect of Protestant Europe's response to the biblical language of poverty, however, is instructive when considering the view(s) of poverty held by their Baptistic heirs.

The Roman view of poverty, by the turn of the sixteenth century, had accreted doctrines as diverse as charity, vocation, salvation, and the church. To reform a church, and a view of salvation, rooted in institutional poverty, meant that the issue of poverty was not merely "moral," but theological to the core. The good work of giving alms, for example, was a crucial part of Roman piety. It also meant that the reformers found themselves playing a bit of three-dimensional chess as they worked to disentangle this theological amalgam, with each "move" in any one area of doctrine impacting other doctrines in unexpected ways. Luther, for example, seems to have begun with a clearer view of what an evangelical response to poverty must *avoid* (i.e. making physical destitution spiritually meritorious) than of how exactly he should fill in the details on this question. As a result, as Bonni Pattison has recently shown, his treatment of the biblical language of poverty is revisited and revised across his career.[4]

Luther initially rejected a socio-economic interpretation of the language of poverty. In his *Dictata* of 1513–1515, the "poor man" of the Psalms was one whose mind was set on spiritual things, who was humbled before the holy majesty of God, who cried out to be filled with the bread of God's word. The "rich," by contrast, were those consumed with carnal desires.[5] In Luther's commentary

---

[2] Matthew Bingham argues that a better term than "Particular Baptist" would be "baptistic Congregationalists." See Matthew Bingham, *Orthodox Radicals: Baptist Identity in the English Revolution* (Oxford: Oxford University Press, 2019).

[3] Carter Lindberg and Lee Wandel have called attention to the theological posture the magisterial reformers carried toward wealth and poverty. Carter Lindberg, *Beyond Charity: Reformation Initiatives for the Poor* (Minneapolis: Fortress Press, 1993); Lee Palmer Wandel, *Always Among Us: Images of the Poor in Zwingli's Zurich* (Cambridge: Cambridge University Press, 1990). Bonnie Pattison, in focusing on Calvin, has helpfully and thoroughly placed the reformer's positions in conversation with the great tradition. See Bonnie Pattison, *Poverty in the Theology of John Calvin* (Eugene, OR: Wipf & Stock, 2006).

[4] Pattison, *Poverty in the Theology of John Calvin*, 82–101.

[5] Lee Brummel, "Luther and the Biblical Language of Poverty," *Ecumenical Review* 32.1 (1980): 43–44. While Luther spoke frequently in these lectures of his life as a monk, he never identified Scripture's language

on Romans (1516–1517), however, the language of poverty was taken according to its plain and literal sense. The Ninety-Five Theses likewise demonstrate a concern for the physical welfare of the poor. Thesis forty-three, for example, asserted that "Christians are to be taught that he who gives to the poor or lends to the needy does a better deed than he who buys indulgences."[6] Similarly, the forty-fifth thesis warned: "Christians are to be taught that he who sees a needy man and passes him by, yet gives his money for indulgences, does not buy papal indulgences but God's wrath."[7] Luther had begun to call the church, as he would continue to do in his debate with John Eck (1486–1543), not to sanctify poverty for the good of the rich but to work toward abolishing it for the sake of the poor.

Around 1519, Luther used his commentary on the Psalms to gloss the "poor" as our "neighbor," narrowing the word's purview to specify fellow Christians under the cross. Luther's aim at this point was to deploy the biblical language of poverty in the battle over the identity of the true church. The true church was indeed a poor church—an oppressed minority, persevering without recourse to the wealth, power, or privilege evident in the Roman institution.[8] In a final shift, in the aftermath of the Peasants' War (1534–1535), as Luther's exegesis de-emphasized his theology of the cross, he took the language of poverty again to address the temporal situation faced by the poor. His commentary on Psalm eighty-two (1530) identified a magistrate who "made the cause of the poor his own" as the greatest blessing a lord could bestow, after promoting the preaching of the pure gospel.[9]

The somewhat fluid nature of Luther's definition of poverty appears reasonable when set against the massive reformation project he increasingly confronted. It also provides important context for this study. Indeed, there are echoes of each of Luther's positions as Particular Baptists exegete the significance of wealth and poverty across their own efforts to further reform the church. The

---

of poverty with making, or keeping, his monastic vows. Nor did he assign any spiritual merit to poverty as a condition, or to charity as an act.

[6] Timothy J. Wengert, ed., "[The 95 Theses or] Disputation for Clarifying the Power of Indulgences, 1517," in *The Annotated Luther: Volume 1 The Roots of Reform*, ed. Timothy J. Wengert (Minneapolis, MN: Fortress, 2015), 40.

[7] Wengert, ed., "[The 95 Theses or] Disputation for Clarifying the Power of Indulgences, 1517," 40.

[8] Brummel, "Luther on Poverty," 49. In his *On the Councils of the Church* (1539), Luther lists seven marks of the true church, including her physical or financial weakness. See Paul W. Robinson, ed., "On the Councils and the Church, 1539," in *The Annotated Luther: Volume 3 Church and Sacraments*, ed. Paul W. Robinson (Minneapolis, MN: Fortress, 2016), 317–444.

[9] Jaroslav Pelikan, ed., *Luther's Works*. Volume 13, Selected Psalms II (St. Louis, MO: Concordian, 1956), 56.

Roman link between poverty and ecclesiology, deeply embedded as it was, meant for Luther that reformation in the one required reformation in the other. As Baptists labored to extend this reformation, they joined an ongoing project to (re)define the biblical imagery of wealth and poverty, as well as its appointed impact on personal piety and public worship.

*Spiritual poverty in Bunyan's Pilgrim's Progress*
John Bunyan (1628–1688) published the first part of his *Pilgrim's Progress* in 1678, soon after his initial release from Bedfordshire county prison. The book's treatment of poverty, as with so many aspects of evangelical piety, exerted a massive influence over the Nonconformist imagination. In Bunyan's allegory, poverty is imaged chiefly as a spiritual condition common to all men, a miserable inability that precludes self-rescue from the City of Destruction. Beginning to dream, Bunyan sees "a man, clothed with raggs … [with] a great burden upon his back."[10] The following descriptions of this "poor pilgrim" blended nicely with the ideas of circumstantial and spiritual woe. Further, the characteristics of physical poverty were deployed to present the wretched need of the soul apart from grace. This approach endured to the end of the book. As Hopeful prepares for his final interview he is helped to pray, "such a poor sinner as I am, … Lord take therefore this opportunity; and magnify thy grace in the salvation of my soul."[11]

The spiritual definition of poverty—man is poor in sin and God is rich in grace—dominates Bunyan's work. Still, as an extended meditation on the Christian life, the book afforded sufficient space for Bunyan to address the relationship between physical poverty (or plenty) and piety with some nuance. For example, at the house of the Interpreter, Christian witnessed a contest between Passion and Patience. The lesson learned, as Passion requested "a bag of treasure, and poured it down at his feet," yet then impoverished himself by having "lavished all away," was that spiritual rewards were more to be desired than worldly gain.[12] Patience chose the better, if the latter part; worth the wait because heaven's riches carried incomparable, and indeed inexhaustible value.

Significantly, the contrast between Passion and Patience, however sharp, did not translate into a suspicion of physical comfort or the repudiation of earthly prosperity. On the contrary, Christian was next shown a sumptuous palace, and his host approved his aspiration to join those upon the ramparts, arrayed as they were in cloth of gold. Not long after, Christian had his own

---

[10] John Bunyan, *The Pilgrim's Progress from this World to That which is to Come*, eds. James Blanton Wharey, and Roger Sharrock, 2nd ed. (Oxford: Clarendon, 1960), 8.

[11] Bunyan, *Pilgrim's Progress*, 142.

[12] Bunyan, *Pilgrim's Progress*, 31.

rags replaced by "fine raiment" as his burden was rolled away. Going on, he was welcomed into a stately house built by the Lord of the Hill, whose ample accommodations, presided over by Piety and Charity, included fine food and spacious rooms, all provided for "the relief and security of pilgrims."[13] These were physical images of surpassing spiritual realities to be sure, but we should not miss the way Bunyan blended precisely these two levels of application together in the pious imagination. Financial comfort did not follow from faith, but neither were the two inimical in the Christian life.

In fact, the emphasis in Bunyan's allegory at this point accords well with the Particular Baptist view of temporal goods as it was transmitted through a contemporary catechism. In *A Brief Instruction in the Principles of Christian Religion* (1695), question eighty-five explained that the tenth commandment required, "full contentment with our own condition, with a right and charitable frame of Spirit toward our neighbor and all that is his."[14] This is the contentment personified in Bunyan's Patience. But it was not the contentment of an ascetic. The same catechism explicated the eighth commandment to *require* "the lawful procuring, and furthering the wealth and outward estate of ourselves and others," going on to proscribe "whatsoever doth, or may, unjustly hinder our own, or our neighbor's wealth, or outward estate."[15] Short pages later, in the exposition of the Lord's Prayer, the catechism interpreted the fourth petition to ask, "that of God's free gift, we may receive a competent portion of the good things of this life, and enjoy his blessing with them."[16]

Far from an inverse relationship between funds and faithfulness, therefore, the growth of one's outward estate and the enjoyment of the good things of this life could be a means of sustaining Christians on their pilgrimage to the Celestial City. Money was a friend in Bunyan's story therefore, unless and until it overstepped a ministerial role and attempted to play the master; that is, when it distracted pilgrims from the proper end of their journey by rivaling the value of heavenly glory. Three such scenes stand out in the story, with the subtlety of mammon's deception increasing each time, as does the ferocity of Bunyan's censure.

In the first scene, the market of Vanity Fair was so flagrantly vacuous that it had little power to beguile the pilgrims as they passed through. Christian and

---

[13] Bunyan, *Pilgrim's Progress*, 46.

[14] *A Brief Instruction in the Principles of Christian Religion: Agreeable to the Confession of Faith, put forth by the Elders and Brethren of Many Congregations of Christians, (Baptized upon Profession of Their Faith) in London and the Country; Owning the Doctrine of Personal Election, and Final Perseverance*, 5th ed. (London, 1695), 17.

[15] *A Brief Instruction in the Principles of Christian Religion*, 16.

[16] *A Brief Instruction in the Principles of Christian Religion*, 22.

Faithful simply "put their fingers in their ears, and cry out, *Turn away mine eyes from beholding vanity*; and look upwards, signifying that their trade and traffick was in heaven."[17] Vanity Fair could threaten to detain their bodies, but it's crass consumerism could not deceive the affections of their hearts.

In the second scene, as Christian journeyed on, he was pursued by a subtler temptation. A Mr. By-ends from the town of Fair-speech, a "wealthy place," opined that religion was profitable so long as it advanced his overarching commitment to "secure my life and estate."[18] As his companion Mr. Hold-the-world clarified, "I like that religion best, that will stand with the security of God's good blessings unto us; for who can imagin[e] that is ruled by his reason, since God has bestowed upon us the good things of this life, but that he would have us keep them for his sake?"[19] For these men, religion was a means of serving their temporal profit, to the point of feigning religious interest where doing so achieved financial advantage.

This perspective was such a perversion—a prostitution—of the proper relationship between money and piety that "even a babe in religion" must reject it. Bunyan's Christian recognized that "hypocrites, hypocrites, devils and witches" alone were of such an opinion. It was one thing to welcome the comfort and increase of our worldly estate as it served our journey home. It was quite another to install mammon as the north star of our pilgrimage. Calculating value according to a very different economy, Christian exhorted his companions to "own religion in his rags, as well as in his silver slippers."[20]

A third confrontation sought to undermine just this confidence in religion's intrinsic value. A new traveler, Shame, insisted that religion's worth ought to be mirrored in the number of "the mighty, rich, or wise" who joined the pilgrims on the road.[21] Such a sorry company as Shame saw before him, therefore, belied their claim regarding the greatness of the kingdom of God. Religion was exposed by the low estate of its adherents to be "a pitiful, low, sneaking business."[22] This opprobrium was common against Baptists in Bunyan's own day, as reflected in Faithful's response. He was stung. The "blood came up in my

---

[17] Bunyan, *Pilgrim's Progress*, 90.

[18] Bunyan, *Pilgrim's Progress*, 98, 102.

[19] Bunyan, *Pilgrim's Progress*, 102.

[20] Bunyan, *Pilgrim's Progress*, 105–106. Augustine's distinction between using (what is temporal) and enjoying (what is eternal) is recognizable here. Treasure may be used to serve the ends of religion, but where treasure is sought for its own sake, as with those who turn aside to Demas' silver mine, it becomes an inescapable snare. Such self-interested travelers are not seen on the pilgrim road again.

[21] Bunyan, *Pilgrim's Progress*, 72.

[22] Bunyan, *Pilgrim's Progress*, 72.

face."[23] Considering the worldly weakness of so many who shared his religious convictions almost overthrew him.

Faithful was steadied by recalling the inverted economy of the kingdom of God. Christ, the supreme wealth "is such a lover of poor pilgrims, that … He had stript himself of his glory … That he might make many pilgrims princes, though by their nature they were beggars born."[24] And because we have been saved by Christ's embrace of our shame, we ourselves embrace this new way of counting value. The pilgrims resolved, therefore, "what God says, is best, though all the men in the world are against it. Seeing then … that the poor man that loveth Christ, is richer than the greatest man in the world that hates him; *Shame* depart, thou art an enemy to my salvation."[25]

These three confrontations illustrate Bunyan's use of poverty as a picture of the spiritual condition a sinner inhabits when striving after salvation in their own strength. Similarly, they capture Bunyan's primary emphasis on wealth as a pointer to the riches of God's grace unto salvation and a surpassing celestial inheritance.[26]

*Accounting for Bunyan's spiritual emphasis*
It is significant to consider the influences that may have inclined John Bunyan toward this primarily spiritual exposition of wealth and poverty. Bunyan was familiar with the constraints of temporal scarcity. As "a tinker and a poor man," he was often absent, attempting to ply a sufficient trade to care for his family. Further, while in jail, he was reduced to making lace for the same reason.[27] Bunyan recalled in his *Grace Abounding to the Chief of Sinners* (1666) that he and his first wife, "came together as poor as poor might be, (not having so much household-stuff as a Dish or Spoon betwixt us both)."[28] Nevertheless, his

---

[23] Bunyan, *Pilgrim's Progress*, 73.

[24] Bunyan, *Pilgrim's Progress*, 52–53.

[25] Bunyan, *Pilgrim's Progress*, 73.

[26] They also remind us that this first half of Bunyan's tale was beset by an underdeveloped ecclesiology; the individual Christian was the focus. Christiana's story, from the lesser-read second half of Bunyan's story, addressed this imbalance as a community of disciples takes center stage. This communal dynamic in the narrative impacts images of poverty and wealth. The mutual care the pilgrims regularly minister to one another proved crucial for their endurance unto final salvation. And this care often took the form of meeting physical, temporal needs within the company, acknowledging such ministry to be a worthy aspect of Christian discipleship.

[27] The description is taken from Christopher Hill, *A Tinker and a Poor Man: John Bunyan and His Church* (New York; London: W.W. Norton, 1990).

[28] John Bunyan, *Grace Abounding to the Chief of Sinners and The Pilgrim's Progress from this World to that which is to come*, ed. Roger Sharrock (London: Oxford University Press, 1966), 10.

wife brought two religious books as her dowry, one of which was Arthur Dent's (1552–1607) *The Plain Man's Pathway to Heaven* (1601).[29] Dent's book included lengthy sections on the crushing oppression the poor often suffered at the hands of the rich. In life, therefore, as in letters, Bunyan was a man acquainted with what poverty entailed for families like his. What accounts, therefore, for his spiritual emphasis in the *Pilgrim's Progress*?

Lotte Mulligan and Judith Richards point to one possible answer; the deep-seated assumption in mid-seventeenth century England that poverty was a problem outstripping the resources of private charity.[30] Thus, healing the "canker" of poverty required public legislation. Mulligan and Richards survey the period of the Commonwealth (1649–1660) and find that, for all the novelty of those years, "the problem of the poor [continued to operate] well within the framework of an established discourse about poverty."[31] To their point, the Rump Parliament passed an act on May 7, 1649, which offered an entirely conventional response to the problem of the poor in terms of the social assumptions underlying their acts and provisions.[32] Even radical proposals, like Peter Chamberlen's (1601–1683) *Poore Mans Advocate*, which urged that the crown, royalist, and church lands be used to employ the poor, continued to operate with traditional moral categories for the (deserving and undeserving) poor, as well as granting priority to a civic response.[33]

Bunyan, therefore, would have seen poor-relief increase during the civil wars. Serving in the New Model Army from 1644 to 1647, he would have been exposed to a variety of such discussions and proposals. He also would have seen, as Ronald Herland discovered in his study of parishes in and around London during this time, public assistance during these years outstripp private

---

[29] Arthur Dent, *The Plainemans Path-way to Heaven: Wherein euery man may cleerely see whether he shall be saved or damned* (London, 1601). Dent's devotional work was exceedingly popular, already in its 25th edition by 1640. Poverty continued, as it had long done, to be so extensive that it was treated both as morally offensive—a cancer on the body politic—and a threat to the established order of things. See A.L. Beier, *The Problem of the Poor in Tudor and Early Stuart England* (London: Lancaster Pamphlets, 1983), 24. The other religious book Bunyan's first wife brought was Lewis Bayly's (1575–1631) *The Practice of Piety* (1612). For Bunyan's mention in *Grace Abounding*, see Bunyan, *Grace Abounding and Pilgrim's Progress*, 10.

[30] Lotte Mulligan, and Judith Richards, "A 'Radical' Problem: The Poor and the English Reformers in the Mid-Seventeenth Century," *Journal of British Studies* 29.2 (1990): 118–146.

[31] Mulligan and Richards, "The 'Radical' Problem," 123.

[32] "May 1649: An Act for the Relief and Imployment of the Poor, and the Punishment of Vagrants, and other disorderly Persons, within the City of London, and the Liberties thereof," in *Acts and Ordinances of the Interregnum, 1642–1660*, eds. C.H. Firth, and R.S. Rait (London: His Majesty's Stationary Office, 1911), 104–110.

[33] Peter Chamberlen, *The Poore Mans Advocate, or England's Samaritan Pouring Oyle and Wyne into the Wounds of the Nation* (London, 1649).

charity by at least a factor of three.[34] It seems reasonable to assume that Bunyan would have been familiar with these conventional attitudes and their public outworkings. Further, while in prison, Bunyan and his family were reliant on private charity. As a pastor, he regularly strategized how to care for "the poor" not only in general but also for specific needs embodied in his congregation. He also ministered, as a dissenter, which placed him outside the parish social-relief networks. Bunyan engaged this issue, in other words, with a local or a personal horizon of concern.

Significantly, Bunyan's role as a dissenting pastor included the perennial need to distinguish his brand of Baptists from other perceived sowers of blasphemy and abuse.[35] It was this need to present the Particular Baptists as "not that kind of radical" that best explains his reticence to picture the alleviation of *physical* poverty as a constituent part of the Christian life. The example of Abiezer Coppe (1619–1672) illuminates the challenge facing dissenters like Bunyan on this issue. Coppe, a Baptist-turned Ranter, rose to prominence as a critic of the hypocrisy rampant in prevailing approaches to charity. By 1650, however, Coppe was condemned by the Parliament for the incendiary techniques he used to gain attention. He was, at the same time, disowned by the Baptists because, as J.F. McGregor recognized, Coppe's methods fit too neatly into the contemporary narrative that the slippery slope of sectarian theology led to the disintegration of social order.[36] Particular Baptists, therefore, had to add charity to a growing list of issues on which they need to guard themselves against guilt by association in the public mind. Given his own incarceration, Bunyan would have been especially sensitive to this need. He was, accordingly, content to have Christian take up the comforting scroll of God's great and very precious spiritual promises rather than the "fiery flying roll" of Coppe's social harangue.

---

[34] Ronald Herland, "Poor Relief in London during the English Revolution," *Journal of British Studies* 18.2 (1979): 30–51.

[35] Seventeenth-century Baptists were often accused, in J.F. McGregor's words, as the "Fount of All Heresy." J.F. McGregor, "The Baptists: Fount of All Heresy" in *Radical Religion in the English Revolution*, ed. J.F. McGregor and B. Reay (Oxford: Oxford University Press, 1984), 23. McGregor's title is modeled on the Presbyterian Robert Bailie's work, *Anabaptisme, the true Fountaine of Independency, Brownies, Antinomy, Familisme, and most of the other errors which for the time doe trouble the Church of England* (London, 1647).

[36] J.F. McGregor, "The Baptists: Fount of All Heresy," 46, 60. Both Coppe's works, *A Fiery Flying Roll: A Word from the Lord to All the Ones of the Earth, Whom This May Concerne: Being the Last Warning Piece at the Dreadfull Day of Judgement* (London, 1650) and *A Second Fiery Flying Roule: To All the Inhabitants of the Earth; Specially to the Rich Ones* (London, 1650) were condemned by Parliament as blasphemous and were ordered burned.

*The General Assembly: Poverty and
Gospel potential among the Particular Baptists*

Emerging from Bunyan's dreamscape to the demands of a fledgling institution at the end of the seventeenth century, Particular Baptists needed a way to meet financial needs among their fellow pilgrims, and to do so in a way that embodied their ecclesiological convictions. Part of their answer, a book-length work attributed to Benjamin Keach (1640–1704), was circulated in 1689 prior to the inaugural General Assembly of that year.[37] Building from a sermon by Nehemiah Coxe (d. 1689), Keach's *Gospel Minister's Maintenance Vindicated* argued the biblical duty of Baptist churches to provide their pastors with adequate financial support.[38]

Significantly, this central claim was able to assume a Baptist consensus regarding the Christian responsibility to care for the poor. The "given" of Christian charity was then contrasted with the congregation's superior obligation to provide for their minister. If the first act was charity, the second was Christian duty. Crucially, both claims were grounded in aspects of a distinctly Baptist polity, shedding light on the way early Particular Baptists in London conceived of poverty and their response to it.

Keach's *Gospel Minister's Maintenance Vindicated* began, perhaps surprisingly for dissenters, by agreeing with the Church of England that individual believers retained "right, title, and possession" over their own goods.[39] Whatever was meant by the biblical call for "every man … liberally to give alms to the poor," therefore, scripture does not endorse the earlier communalism of continental Anabaptism. Neither did it justify the Anglican overreach in the national tax, used to support ministers and fill coffers for charity.[40]

Where was the path forward between these opposing abuses? Forsaking the poor to own the Erastians was not an option; "Will you disown your duty to the poor saints, and not relieve them, but object and say, 'tis too much like the national practice?"[41] The answer was no. Neither institutional nor individual

---

[37] [Keach,] *The Gospel Minister's Maintenance Vindicated. Wherein, a Regular Ministry in the Churches, is First Asserted, and the objections against a Gospel Maintenance for ministers, Answered. Also, the Dignity, Necessity, Difficulty, Use and Excellency of the Ministry of Christ is Opened. Likewise, the Nature and Weightiness of that Sacred Work and Office Clearly Evinc'd* (London, 1689). The authorship of this pamphlet has been debated, as others have argued that Hanserd Knollys (1599?–1691) was the author.

[38] Nehemiah Coxe, *A Sermon Preached at the Ordinatoin* [sic] *of an Elder and Deacons in a Baptized Congregation in London* (London, 1681). The book also makes frequent use of Matthew Poole's (1624–1679) *A Commentary on the Holy Bible* (London, 1685).

[39] [Keach,] "Advertisement," in *Gospel Minister's Maintenance Vindicated*, [leaf 12].

[40] [Keach,] "Advertisement," in *Gospel Minister's Maintenance Vindicated*, [leaf 12].

[41] [Keach,] *Gospel Minister's Maintenance Vindicated*, 89.

abuse—as when one seeks "to come into your communion meerly for a maintenance"—released churches from accountability to the commands of Christ.[42] What was needed was a category to motivate Christian liberality that could account for both the clear commands of scriptures and the voluntary nature of Baptist ecclesiology.

For Keach, that category was stewardship. Keach asked, "Hath the Lord made you any other than stewards of your worldly things?"[43] Thus, for Christians, the business of this life was to "improve their Masters money" by "giving to everyone their due portion, according to the Masters order."[44] Thus, it is God's will, as revealed in the scriptures, to call Christians to "communicate to others your worldly or carnal things: we mean to the poor saints and ministers of the gospel."[45]

From the time of John Smyth (c.1554–c.1612), this "communication of carnal things" had been entrusted to deacons as ministers of corporate stewardship. Smyth described deacons as "officers occupied about the works of mercy respecting the body or outward man."[46] To this end, male deacons were charged to "collect and distribute with simplicity the churches treasury according to the churches necessities, and the Saints occasions."[47] Because of the independent nature of Baptist polity, however, the exercise of this stewardship was veiled behind the church books of discrete congregations. Denominating what faithfulness to Christ's poor looked like, therefore, was "left to the wisdom and consideration of the church."[48]

Nevertheless, an active deaconate did not exhaust the definition of Christian stewardship. A congregation's charity was to be surpassed by their faithful maintenance of their minister. Motivated by polity, Baptists understood that it was their duty to pay the minister, who was not only worthy as a gospel minister, but had been called by the congregation. Exercising this act of church power included the corollary that, in calling him "off from other business," the church thereby committed to provide for his maintenance.[49] Such a provision

---

[42] [Keach,] *Gospel Minister's Maintenance Vindicated*, 106.

[43] [Keach,] *Gospel Minister's Maintenance Vindicated*, 36–37.

[44] [Keach,] *Gospel Minister's Maintenance Vindicated*, 122–123.

[45] [Keach,] *Gospel Minister's Maintenance Vindicated*, 37.

[46] John Smyth, *Principles and Inferences Concerning the Visible Church*, in *The Works of John Smyth, Fellow of Christ's College, 1594–8*, ed. W.T. Whitley (Cambridge: Cambridge University Press, 1915), 1:259.

[47] Smyth, *Principles and Inferences Concerning the Visible Church*, 1:259.

[48] [Keach,] *Gospel Minister's Maintenance Vindicated*, 196.

[49] [Keach,] *Gospel Minister's Maintenance Vindicated*, 78.

was not to be at the level of mere subsistence, as seemed too often to be the case.[50] Instead, "God would not have his faithful ministers want any good thing to make their lives comfortable to them."[51] The aim was not to make wealthy pastors but to release the spiritual vibrancy in Baptist churches that would result from ministers with salaries sufficient to enable them to invest wholly in their work.[52]

Like Bunyan, Keach wrote about ministerial support within the framework of recent suffering. Thus, while he rejoiced in "the present liberty" enjoyed after the Act of Toleration in 1689, and thanked God for the "respite from our former sufferings," Keach urged Baptists to "improve [their] liberty" by laboring for the "great and glorious work of the churches deliverance."[53] The leading edge of this labor, according to the *Gospel Minister's Maintenance Vindicated*, was a fundamental shift in congregational posture from one of defensive endurance to forward-leaning advance. Speaking plainly, the book announced that taking advantage of this propitious season required improving the quality of ministers called by Baptist congregations, despite the commensurate increase in the church's financial obligation.

In a piercing bit of self-evaluation, the authors wrote: "some of the churches seem to be contented with any, nay, the meanest gifts that are amongst them, provided they can have them without any charge, rather than that they will

---

[50] For instance, Keach pointed out that it was "rare to see a pastor of our churches to abound in riches" ([Keach,] *Gospel Minister's Maintenance Vindicated*, 90). Even in 1812, a letter addressed to the editor of the *Baptist Magazine* lamented that "there are no ministers that are so ill-provided for as Baptist ministers" (S.K.L., "Reply to the Enquiries of ATOI Respecting the Deficiency of Pastors," *Baptist Magazine* [September 1812], 366–371).

[51] [Keach,] *Gospel Minister's Maintenance Vindicated*, 24. The conviction was repeated a few pages later, "They take care to provide bread for your souls, and of right therefore should live upon your charge, and you ought to see that neither they nor their families want bread, or anything necessary for their bodies" ([Keach,] *Gospel Minister's Maintenance Vindicated*, 35).

[52] There would be times, of course, when a minister would remain poor. "If the congregation be poor, and there is no help to be had, then their minister must and ought to be content to be poor with them" ([Keach,] *Gospel Minister's Maintenance Vindicated*, 84). The author wondered aloud, "How many there are among professors that live in this world as if there were no truth in the report of that which is to come, and have the meanest esteem of the most necessary means of salvation, viz. the word and ordinances of Christ, and a gospel ministry? Some can expend perhaps an hundred pounds per annum, more or less, for ornaments or delights to adorn a frail carcass, but will grudge half so much for the poor saints, or to the support of the worship of the gospel" ([Keach,] *Gospel Minister's Maintenance Vindicated*, 80).

[53] [Keach,] *Gospel Minister's Maintenance Vindicated*, 1, 99. They describe this newfound freedom thus: "The case, blessed be the Lord, is much altered: you may come now into any town and none dare forbid you (if any one will but entertain you) to preach the gospel" ([Keach,] *Gospel Minister's Maintenance Vindicated*, 93). Following chapters are punctuated with reminders of "the storms of persecution [that] were upon us," hindering the work of church planting and soul harvesting until God "hath done great things for us, and hath opened a mighty door" ([Keach,] *Gospel Minister's Maintenance Vindicated*, 93, 102).

seek out, and endeavor for an able and honorable ministry, because of that great expense and cost they fear then they shall be at."[54] Such a mindset of making-do was a holdover from darker days, when gatherings were covert and few ministers could access adequate training.[55] But it was decidedly out of step with the opportunities afforded by their new situation. Indeed, to retain this mindset amid the opportunities provided by toleration risked the "blast" of divine displeasure. The spiritual cost of settling for "mean gifts" far outweighed the financial cost of calling men equipped to rightly handle the word of God.

More positively, the book sought at this point to impart a rich vision of pastoral ministry, to stir the reader's imagination regarding what could now be in Baptist churches. This section of the book is sufficiently compelling to quote at some length:

> True, we may perhaps have preachers … but is it fit, think you, to call such to preach publicly, who have scarcely one hour's time to prepare themselves for the work? … What would you have poor men to do, that have (may be) no time to spare to give themselves up to the study of the Scriptures, nor no useful books and proper helps to improve them in their study: or…[have not sufficient] leisure from their worldly business to read and meditate upon the Word, so as well to digest what they have to deliver to the people.
>
> A little knowledge and study, 'tis true, may furnish a man with such a discourse as may please some weak Christians that judge of a sermon by the loudness of the voice and affectionate sentences, or can fancy themselves to be fed with good doctrine when, perhaps, 'tis but with the ashes of jingling words and cadency of terms. He that will do the souls of his people good, and approve himself a pastor after God's own heart, must endeavor to feed them with knowledge and understanding, … and such an opening of the mind of God from the Scripture … is not to be expected but from him that labors in his study as well as in the pulpit.[56]

Such a vision—churches that so prize the increasing quality of preaching and pastoral care that they gladly provide not only for their own minister but also contribute toward competent ministers serving impoverished areas—was the seed of a conviction that grew into the Particular Baptist Fund at the General Assembly of 1689. In reliably Baptist fashion, the response to a kingdom-need

---

[54] [Keach,] *Gospel Minister's Maintenance Vindicated*, 67.

[55] The illiteracy of Baptist preachers was a common slur by Oxbridge Anglicans.

[56] [Keach,] *Gospel Minister's Maintenance Vindicated*, 58–61.

among their various churches was cooperation.[57]

On the second day of this inaugural Assembly (September 5, 1689), delegates "considered, debated and concluded, that a publick fund, or stock was necessary."[58] The purpose of the voluntary fund was threefold: to provide competent ministers for "those churches not able to maintain their own ministry;" to send ministers to preach, "both in city and in country" where the gospel has yet to be preached; and to provide ministerial training [in Latin, Greek, and Hebrew] for church members who "are disposed for Study" and "have an inviting gift."[59] The strengthening of the church required churches to place a financial premium on cultivating and maintaining high caliber gospel ministers.[60] The fund thus formed the theme of the General Assembly's communication in 1690, again 1691, and at their final gathering 1692.

In sum, Particular Baptists at the close of the seventeenth century grappled with poverty as a physical reality. Images of indigency retained a place in their spiritual poetics, but they devoted considerable energy to equipping their congregations for faithful financial stewardship. This stewardship required churches to exercise charity toward the poor in their midst—many of whom would have, through their membership in an independent congregation, forfeited the benefits of the parish welfare system. What is more, they did so without first distinguishing between "deserving" or "undeserving" recipients.[61] Never-

---

[57] Cooperation characterized Baptists of all stripes. The General Assembly of General Baptists in England, for example, supported sister works in South Carolina by raising funds to purchase books (7 pounds 12 shillings in 1702) and then ministers to resource the churches there (100 pounds sterling in 1757). See W.T. Whitley, ed., *Minutes of the General Assembly of the General Baptist Churches in England* (London: Kingsgate Press, 1910).

[58] *A Narrative of the Proceedings of the General Assembly of Divers Pastors, Messengers and Ministring [sic]-Brethren of the Baptized Churches, met together in London, from Septemb. 3. to 12. 1689, from divers parts of England and Wales: Owning the Doctrine of Personal Election, and final Perseverance* (London, 1689), 10.

[59] *Narrative of the Proceedings of the General Assembly*, 12.

[60] The General Assembly of 1690 recognized: "as it is our privilege to be in a capacity to do good in our generation, so it is our duty, and will be our crown and glory to lay out ourselves and our talents—not only spiritually but also temporally—speedily, while the power is in our hands, and faithfully, to the utmost we can…O that God would give us great souls disposed to do great things for him" (*A Narrative of the Proceedings of the General Assembly of the Elders and Messengers of the Baptized Churches sent from divers parts of England and Wales, which began in London the 9th of June, and ended the 16th of the same, 1690* [London, 1690], 4–5).

[61] The author of *Gospel Minister's Maintenance Vindicated* exhorted individual church members to liberality. Riches are not viewed as problematic, provided they give "as they are able." The harsh words are reserved for those whose "hardness of heart" is attested by the fact that they would spend "an hundred pounds per annum, more or less, for ornaments or delights to adorn a frail carcase [sic], but will grudg [sic] half so much for the poor saints, or to the support of the worship of the gospel, and his sinking interest" ([Keach,]

theless, the dominant emphasis in congregational stewardship fastened on the financial needs of their pastors. This focus was owing to Particular Baptist craving for the quality of ministry that could only come as pastors pursued their vocation with undivided attention.

*Poverty in the theology and hymnody of Anne Dutton*
Born in 1692, the year of the final General Assembly, Anne Dutton (née Williams, 1692–1765) drank deeply from the "clear stream of the pure Gospel" flowing from Particular Baptist pulpits.[62] Dutton valued public worship to an exceptional degree. "Gospel-worship," she wrote in 1737, "is a glorious way wherein God and his people walk together."[63] The glory of this communion was its divine appointment as the means by which the "poor are satisfied with bread" (after the promise of Ps 132:15) and those in distress are "caused to drink and forget their poverty" (from Prov 31:7).[64] Such an image of public worship as a house of bread for the poor recurs throughout Dutton's tracts, journals, and letters, suggesting itself as a starting point from which to consider her use of the biblical language of wealth and poverty. Dutton's approach privileged biblical promises, and the spiritual realities to which they pointed, as the lens through which she evaluated both the provision and the poverty experienced in this life. What God's word said would be the fixed point of reference by which she responded to what she saw. Dutton acknowledged, for example, that "some prosperity, more or less, our dear Father is pleased to afford all his children."[65] Nevertheless, the saints were, for the most part, "a poor and afflicted people (Zeph 3:12)."[66] This was true on the temporal face of things. There was a second and Scriptural perspective, however, that granted both believing prosperity and believing poverty a more profound richness.

Regarding temporal prosperity, the saints received what Dutton celebrated as "the inside of the blessing" or "the good in the mercy," that is, "God's heart

---

*Gospel Minister's Maintenance Vindicated*, 80).

[62] JoAnn Ford Watson, ed., *Selected Spiritual Writings of Anne Dutton: Eighteenth-Century, British-Baptist, Woman Theologian, Volume 3: Autobiography* (Macon, GA: Mercer University Press, 2006), 47.

[63] JoAnn Ford Watson, ed., *Selected Spiritual Writings of Anne Dutton: Eighteenth-Century, British-Baptist, Woman Theologian. Volume 2: Discourses, Poetry, Hymns, Memoir* (Macon, GA: Mercer University Press, 2004), 15.

[64] Watson, ed., *Selected Spiritual Writings of Anne Dutton*, 2:49.

[65] Watson, ed., *Selected Spiritual Writings of Anne Dutton*, 2:109. There was certainly no suggestion in Dutton that poverty carried intrinsic spiritual value. At her own death, the long-time widow was able to leave houses and lands worth more than 25*l*. per annum, along with a library of choice books, to support ongoing gospel work at Great Gransden.

[66] Watson, ed., *Selected Spiritual Writings of Anne Dutton*, 2:17.

in every favor they enjoy."⁶⁷ It was, accordingly, "a higher joy to a child of God, walking with him in prosperity, that thereby he is enabled to glorify God the more, serve his cause, and be rich in good works, than all the outward advantages which accrue to himself thereby."⁶⁸ The divine fellowship enjoyed through faithful stewardship was the true treasure in temporal wealth. The great part of Dutton's life, however, was lived as a steward not of prosperity but of what she termed "afflictive providence."⁶⁹ Here too spiritual reality enriched and transformed temporal experience. To take one item from a catalog of adversity, in 1732 the Duttons moved to Great Gransden where Benjamin Dutton was called to two congregations, both of which were "in low estate" and "without supply."⁷⁰ Benjamin admirably filled both pulpits, eventually consolidating the congregations. But it was not until 1743 that the church experienced sufficient growth to construct both a new meeting house and a new residence for their minister and his wife.

Dutton did not directly reveal her response to the financial constraint she and her husband endured during this time. We do get a glimpse, however, in a letter she wrote to a "dear brother," called to a similar work "among the Lord's … poor people," in 1735. In the letter, Dutton exhorted him "not to be discouraged from abiding with them because of their low estate." Significantly, the hope Dutton offered this young shepherd was that, "the Lord Jesus is with you, even among the myrtle trees in the bottom," and "when God doth arise to have mercy upon Zion, he usually makes his servants to take pleasure in her stones, and favor her dust."⁷¹ In other words, when both pastor and people find themselves in the circumstantial "dust" of Psalm 102 or the financially depressed "valley" of Zechariah 1:8, they can expect the spiritual richness of Christ's presence precisely there. It is when we stand "in the furnace of affliction" that we are "favored with [our Father's] presence therein."⁷²

---

⁶⁷ Which is why "Prosperity would be comfortless to [the saints] if God was not with them there." The wicked, by contrast, were blind to the fountain from which their blessings flow, and so "boast of their wealth as if gotten by their own hand (Ps 49:6)." Watson, ed., *Selected Spiritual Writings of Anne Dutton*, 2:33.

⁶⁸ Watson, ed., *Selected Spiritual Writings of Anne Dutton*, 2:34.

⁶⁹ Watson, ed., *Selected Spiritual Writings of Anne Dutton*, 3:128. High profile afflictions in Dutton's life included the death of her first husband, four years of separation from her second husband, Benjamin, as he traveled to America in 1743, only to perish on his return voyage in 1747, with both bereavements being compounded by her own childlessness, and several illnesses "unto death."

⁷⁰ The fact that these conditions, the very ones that had precipitated the rise of the Particular Baptist Fund at the end of the previous century, persisted into Dutton's time makes the dissolution of the Particular Baptist General Assembly, and with it the Fund, all the more lamentable.

⁷¹ Watson, ed., *Selected Spiritual Writings of Anne Dutton*, 2:3.

⁷² Watson, ed., *Selected Spiritual Writings of Anne Dutton*, 2:98.

In reflecting on this biblical imagery, surely drawn from texts that fed her own soul during the lean years at Great Gransden, it is worth considering the fact that Dutton did not direct her friend's attention to the hope of her own (now improving) situation. Why might she fill her letter, and the tract it introduced on walking with God, with the language of Scriptural, rather than biographical, encouragement? What could account for her focus on the spiritual reality in every temporal experience? The best answer is that Dutton's perspective on wealth and poverty had been subsumed under the defining labor of her Christian life, trusting scripture's truth rather than resting in her own "sense" of the situation. This formative discipline emerged early in her *Autobiography*, as Dutton described her growth into "the Way of Faith, when I had not spiritual sense." Before this, she often suffered "soul plunges" as circumstances roiled her confidence that God was, and was to her, who he said he would be. Assurance ebbed and flowed like a cruel tide. Gradually, however, "the Blessed Spirit taught me to … foot it by faith when I had not the prop of spiritual sense to lean on."[73] As she learned to trust "in the Lord, and not in [her] frames," she was strengthened to rejoice in the God of her salvation, "even where the streams of sensible enjoyment failed."[74] This spiritual habit, reading temporal experience through the lens of biblical promises, recurred across her own testimony and was a note frequently sounded in her exhortations to others.

The significance of this habit becomes apparent when we recognize that it formed not only the opening movement of her autobiography, but her final suffering as well, thus framing her life's story.[75] Over the final year of her life, Dutton endured a growth in her throat that made it increasingly painful, and eventually impossible, to eat or drink. Her experiences during this illness could, at times, resemble those of acute poverty. Friends reported her speaking often, for example, "under the exercise of an empty … stomach," exclaiming, "my poor stomach, how it does crave! It prays me to give it something, but I can get nothing to it."[76] Dutton made the poignant connection with poverty overt, taking personal comfort from biblical promises vouchsafed to the poor, "The Lord frequently tells me of his delivering kindness … 'for the oppression of the

---

[73] Watson, ed., *Selected Spiritual Writings of Anne Dutton*, 3:27, 28.

[74] Watson, ed., *Selected Spiritual Writings of Anne Dutton*, 3:27.

[75] Dutton picked it up in the center as well. With a premonition that her husband had drowned, she went to buy newspapers to search for word of his ship. But a Scriptural promise rebuked her unbelief and she laid aside the papers unread, committed to "rejoice greatly in the Lord…'although the fig-tree did not blossom, nor fruit was found in the vine' [verses she took to mean] there being nothing to feed sense." While she was thus trusting, and rejoicing, her husband returned (Watson, ed., *Selected Spiritual Writings of Anne Dutton*, 3:99–100).

[76] Watson, ed., *Selected Spiritual Writings of Anne Dutton*, 2:101.

poor, and for the sighing of the needy, now I will arise, saith the Lord."[77] As her affliction intensified, however, it became clear the kind of deliverance she had in mind. "I was much pleased yesterday, Madam," she comforted a friend, "to think that, after my long natural fast, I should shortly have a most delightful, spiritual, and eternal feast."[78] Such unflagging cheerfulness was no affectation. Here is the key: "you think my affliction very great, and so indeed it is to flesh and sense but ... a thought of giving him glory makes me, at times, lose the smart in that ineffable sweet!"[79] Her life, from first to last, was a growing walk of faith over fear, rooted in scripture and resting in divine promises.[80] Such promises could be reflected, but never exhausted, in a believer's circumstances.

The whole of Dutton's autobiographical and theological writings expressed a profound awareness of the wages of sin, the debt of human depravity, the wealth of free grace, and the inestimable glory of a heavenly inheritance. But it was in her hymns—poetic distillations of favorite theological truths—that Dutton's piety was at its most potent. It is in her hymnody, therefore, that her approach to the biblical language of prosperity and poverty can be most clearly seen for what it is: temporal pointers to spiritual truths that are far more wonderful, and terrible.[81]

Dutton used the language of poverty to lament our spiritual devastation in Adam:

All kinds of death, in sentence/hath pass'd on all men in one;
The first man left the rest in debt/as bankrupts, quite undone.
In this sad case, there's none, alas!/By any means that can;
<u>A ransom give</u> that they may live/so poor is fallen man.[82]

---

[77] Watson, ed., *Selected Spiritual Writings of Anne Dutton*, 2:105.

[78] Dutton continued, "These [biblical promises of deliverance] strengthen my faith, excite my praise, and patience of hope to wait. Mourn not for me, Madam, but rejoice in the Lord, your eternal portion, in whom you are so well provided with all supplies ... that in the most trying of cases you cannot, shall not, want any good thing" (Watson, ed., *Selected Spiritual Writings of Anne Dutton*, 2:105).

[79] Watson, ed., *Selected Spiritual Writings of Anne Dutton*, 2:101.

[80] "Usually, faith got the victory over fears, and laid me to rest in divine promises" (Watson, ed., *Selected Spiritual Writings of Anne Dutton*, 3:99).

[81] Dutton's hymns were written largely for devotional reflection rather than public worship. The various branches of Baptist hymnody may be loosely grouped according to the following scheme: (1) General Baptist hymnody leveraged wealth/reward imagery in their hymns as part of their compelling welcome to whoever would come to Christ, (2) Fifth Monarchists or Radicals used wealth/poverty imagery in their hymns to picture the great inversion/reversal that would accompany the spiritual-social restructuring of society, and (3) Particular Baptists used the imagery of wealth/poverty in their hymns to exalt the superiority of Christ, and the value gained by the saints in Him, in order to encourage resignation under God's hand in this world.

[82] Watson, ed., *Selected Spiritual Writings of Anne Dutton*, 2:223. She copied Shepherd's "Lord I come

In confronting our spiritual bankruptcy, Dutton's aim was to strike our hearts with wonder at the riches of God's gracious response:

> Though Christ was rich in glory great/he laid aside his royal state;
> And with the greatest joy came down/to make our poverty his own.[83]

She was then able to celebrate the result, as adopted sons of God receive a share in an immeasurable inheritance. In her hymn, "God, the Saint's Portion," Dutton writes:

> Oh! What a privilege it is/In Jesus to be blest;
> Saints that can see it for themselves/Do enter into rest.
>
> With favour we are satisfy'd/And full with blessing so;
> Our souls can crave no more than what/Our Father did bestow.
>
> In the eternal covenant/the charter of our bliss;
> Where we, with Christ, are made joint heirs/Of all Jehovah is.
>
> Jehovah freely gave himself/as our eternal all;
> A portion which we could not spend/though bankrupt in the fall.
>
> Here's all our happiness comprised/as in a total sum;
> And hence, as from the fountain-head/the streams of blessing come.
>
> Christ is the treasury of all/the Father's boundless grace;
> And from his fullness saints receive/according to their place.
>
> Jehovah so did give himself/to ev'ry of his heirs;
> That each have all in him, which each/His lot of glory share.
>
> Lord, since thou'rt ours for evermore/fill us with praises high;
> And let us feast on God in Christ/E'en to eternity.[84]

---

extremely poor" into her journal.

[83] Watson, ed., *Selected Spiritual Writings of Anne Dutton*, 2:126.

[84] Watson ed., *Selected Spiritual Writings of Anne Dutton*, 2:197. Dutton also wrote the similarly titled, "The Soul's Joy in God as its Portion," where she comforts herself that "[God] knows, and will supply my wants, How great so e'er they be." See Watson, ed., *Selected Spiritual Writings of Anne Dutton*, 2:239–240.

The proleptic celebration of this feast in spiritual communion, and the invitation for others to take their blood-bought place around this banqueting table, was the chief exercise of Dutton's life and ministry. It was the eternal promise she beheld in every circumstance, making prosperity a pointer to God's yet greater goodness, and making poverty a servant to prepare her heart for glory.

*Conclusion*
This paper began by noting the development, across Luther's career as a reformer, of his understanding of poverty. The cause of this variation in Luther's position was the skein of doctrinal and moral indecencies that had resulted when the Roman church wedded poverty both to her soteriology and her ecclesiology. In attempting to define the evangelical posture on poverty, therefore, Luther often found that clarity on one issue caused confusion on another. His fluid definition of poverty reflected this tension. Given this complexity, the success of Luther's reformation was rooted in his commitment to drive the church to scripture, and derive the preaching and practices of the church from scripture. The Word of God was to be the agent and standard of reformation. Unlike efforts at merely moral reform, which would have either collapsed under the intricacy of an issue like poverty or made themselves obsolete to the degree they were successful, a reformation according to the Word of God endured.

The Particular Baptists of the seventeenth century inherited the reformer's zeal to do full justice to scripture in their congregational life. Specifically, they labored to honor a Bible that has as much to say about loving our neighbor in our temporal stewardship as it does about hoping in God as we anticipate eternal riches. Perhaps the greatest inheritance the Baptists received from the reformers, then, was a commitment to set scripture as the north star of the Christian life. In this way, where doctrine needs ongoing clarification, or our life is out of alignment with our teaching, the reformation of the Church remains on stable footing. As Bonnie Pattison has suggested, Luther succeeded in providing a thoroughgoing Protestant understanding of poverty precisely because the scriptures, not the reform of the Christian life, was his focus.[85] Luther himself recognized this difference; "others have fought over life, but to take on doctrine—that is to grab the goose by the neck. When the Word of God remains pure, even if the quality of life fails us, life is placed in a position to become what it ought to be. That is why everything hinges on the purity of the Word."[86]

---

[85] Pattison, *Poverty in the Theology of John Calvin*, 89.

[86] Luther's quote begins, somewhat uncharitably to his predecessors: "Wycliffe and Huss didn't know this [the distinction between doctrine and life] and attacked [the papacy] for its life. I don't scold myself into becoming good, but I fight over the Word and whether our adversaries teach it in its purity. That doctrine should be attacked—this has never before happened. This is my calling. Others have censured only life, but to treat doctrine is to strike at the most sensitive point, for surely the government and the ministry of the

Getting doctrine right, therefore, laboring to keep the scriptures pure, cannot be seen as a distraction to practical obedience. It is, rather, the only hope that our piety and practice will increasingly come into conformity with Christ. This is hope we take from watching the eighteenth-century Particular Baptists work their way toward a full-orbed and biblical faithful response to poverty.

---

papists are bad. Once we've asserted this, it's easy to say and declare that the life is also bad" (Martin Luther, *Luther's Works Volume 54 Table Talk*, ed. and trans., Theodore G. Tappert [Philadelphia: Fortress Press, 1967], 54:110).

*The Journal of Andrew Fuller Studies*
5 | September 2022

# A bibliography of the writings of John Collett Ryland

Garrett M. Walden

Garrett M. Walden is a PhD student in historical and theological studies at The Southern Baptist Theological Seminary, and a pastor at Grace Heritage Church in Auburn, Alabama.

---

*Introduction*

John Collett Ryland (1723–1792) was a prolific author among the eighteenth-century Particular Baptists. As a pastor and schoolmaster, he was extraordinarily well-read and began publishing his own work early in his ministry. He eventually spent himself into financial hardship to keep the press busy, which prompted both merited criticism and merciful assistance from his friends and family. Writing Ryland's biography in 1835, William Newman said of his beloved mentor's publishing habit, "Mr. Ryland would have done more, had he done less."[1]

Below is an attempt at an exhaustive bibliography of Ryland's confirmed works. I am sure there are more works authored or published by him anonymously, and it is now nearly impossible to confirm him as the author.[2] In com-

---

[1] William Newman, *Rylandiana: Reminiscences Relating to the Rev. John Ryland, A. M. of Northampton. Father of the Late Rev. Dr. Ryland, of Bristol* (London: George Wightman, 1835), 136.

[2] Peter Naylor compiled a similar list with only twenty-six titles attributed to Ryland in his chapter, "John Collett Ryland (1723–1792)," in *The British Particular Baptists: 1638–1910*, ed. Michael A.G. Haykin (Springfield, MO: Particular Baptist Press, 2000), 4:306–310. My list is, to my knowledge, exhaustive. I was assisted by the archivists, Mr. Mike Brealey at Bristol Baptist College and Adam Winters at The Southern Baptist Theological Seminary. I was also helped by the work of W.T. Whitley, *A Baptist Bibliography: Being a Register of the Chief Materials for Baptist History, Whether in Manuscript or in Print, Preserved in Great Britain, Ireland, and the Colonies*, vol. 2 (London: The Kingsgate Press, 1916); Edward C. Starr, *A Baptist Bibliog-*

piling this list, I am indebted to others who have made the attempt before me. Accounting for repetitions, some that are dubiously attributed to Ryland, and some erroneously attributed works of Ryland Jr., the Whitley bibliography accounts for fifty-one titles; the Starr bibliography notes sixty-two titles; and the Wallis checklist records seventy-nine titles. My list contains 121 titles.

Some of the titles listed were published and still exist, and thankfully, many of these works are available digitally in the *Eighteenth Century Collections Online* database or Google Books. Some of these may have been published and are lost or lie unknown in an archive, and some may never have been published at all (but Ryland referred to his intention to publish them). Those documents that I have not acquired digitally are marked with an asterisk.

*Ryland's Theological Works*

1. *List of Baptist Churches in Great Britain; Numbering 200* (1753).[3]
2. "A Contemplation on the Perfections and Glories of Christ," *The Gospel Magazine, or Spiritual Library, Designed to Promote Scriptural Religion* 6 (October 1771): 438–445.[4]
3. *A Demonstration of the Horrid Nature of Sin* (London: John Robinson, Thomas Field, and Edward Dilly, 1755).
4. *The Christian Preacher Delineated* (London: D. Nottage, Ward, Dodsley, Buckland, Robinson, Keith, Field, Dilly, and Law, 1757).[5]
5. "Full Assurance of Faith," *The Gospel Magazine, or Spiritual Library, Designed to Promote Scriptural Religion* 7 (May 1772): 133–139; (May 1772): 216–218.[6]
6. *\*The Evidences of the Truth, Goodness, and Beauty of the Christian Religion*

---

raphy: *Being a register of printed material by and about Baptists; including works written against the Baptists*, vol. 20 (Chester, PA: American Baptist Historical Society, 1953); and P.J. Wallis, *A Check-List of the Writings of John Collett Ryland, 1723-1792* (Newcastle upon Tyne: n.p., 1972). In each of these prior bibliographies, it is not uncommon for works to be misattributed between John Collett Ryland and his son, John Ryland Jr. For the sake of space, I will not often comment where prior bibliographies have erred.

[3] Reprinted in 1845. It was transcribed and republished in Arthur S. Langley, "Baptist Ministers in England about 1750 A.D.," *Transactions of the Baptist Historical Society*, vol. 6 (1918-1919), 138–157.

[4] It is noted as "published" in 1754 in *A Contemplation on the Nature and Evidences of the Divine Inspiration of the Holy Scriptures* (1776).

[5] A version of this treatise was reprinted in parts from August–September 1776 in *The Gospel Magazine, or Treasury of Divine Knowledge, Designed to Promote Experimental Religion* 3 (London, 1776): 345–355, 402–405.

[6] This work is identified as published in 1757 in a letter from James Hervey in Ryland's *The Character of the Rev. James Hervey* (1790).

*for the Use of Youth* (London: T. and J. W. Pasham, 1768).[7]
7. *The Assistance of God to True Christians. The Circular Letter from the Ministers and Messengers assembled at Northampton, May 30 and 31, 1769* (London: Thomas and John Wheler Pasham, 1769).
8. *The Divinity and Names of Our Lord Jesus Christ. In Three Classes. To Which Are Added, the Titles Given Him by the Primitive Fathers of the Christian Church* (London: T. and J. W. Pasham, 1769).
9. *The Evidences of Christianity, Briefly Stated, and the New Testament Proved to be Genuine* (London: J. Buckland, W. Strahan, J. Rivington, R. Baldwin, L. Hawes, W. Clarke, R. Collins, W. Johnston, S. Crowder, T. Longman, B. Law, T. Field, W. Nicoll, and M. Richardson, 1770).[8]
10. *The Scheme of Infidelity Ruined For Ever: or, The Deistical and Socinian Schemes Demonstrated to be Insufficient for the Happiness of Mankind; and the Necessity of the Glorious Gospel to Discover Pardon, Sanctification, and Support in Death* (London: E. and C. Dilly, 1770).
11. *The Student and Preacher: or Advice to Students of Divinity and Young Ministers of the Gospel* (London: E. and C. Dilly, 1770).
12. *A Theological Dictionary Sacred to Religion and Learning: Containing and Explanation of the Terms, and an Account of the Things Signified Thereby, in the Sacred Science of Divinity* (London: E. and C. Dilly, 1770).[9]
13. *The Death-bed Terrors of an Infidel; or, A Modern Freethinker Exemplified in the Last Awful Hours of a Young Gentleman Who Departed from the Principles of Christianity, and Turned Deist. to Which is Added, as a Contrast, the Glorious Salvation of Baron Dyherrn from Infidelity, Who Died in April, 1759* (London: E. and C. Dilly, 1770).
14. *Select Lessons and Orations for the Use of Youth at Boarding-Schools; or, the Productions of Genius and Taste: Containing Some of the First Principles of Natural Religion, Christianity, Natural and Moral Philosophy; and Fine Pieces of History, Eloquence, and Poetry* (London: E. and C. Dilly, 1770).
15. *Contemplations Suited to the Lord's Supper, for the Service of Serious Christians When They Commemorate the Death of Christ: Extracted from the Judicious Dr. Witsius's Admirable Treatise on the Covenants of God with Man* (Northampton: Thomas Dicey, 1770).
16. "Memoirs of the Life and Character of that Most Learned and Judicious Divine Stephen Charnock," *The Gospel Magazine, or Spiritual Library*,

---

[7] This title is listed in the Wallis checklist.

[8] Originally composed in 1749, this is Ryland's abridgement (with his own additions) of Philip Doddridge, *Three Sermons on the Evidences of the Gospel*, 3rd ed. (London: J. Waugh, 1752).

[9] Begun in 1750, this appears to be an evolving document, but only the outline of this work is included at the end of *The Scheme of Infidelity ruined For Ever* (1770). It is unknown if the whole was ever produced.

*Designed to Promote Scriptural Religion* 6 (February–April 1771): 56–61, 113–116, 153–159.

17. "On the Glorious Use and Intent of Prophecy: Or, A Demonstration of the Truth and Divine Inspiration of the Sacred Scriptures, from the Fulfilment of the Prophecies Concerning the Messiah, in Jesus of Nazareth *The Gospel Magazine, or Spiritual Library, Designed to Promote Scriptural Religion* 6 (February–March 1771): 90–92, 120–126.

18. "A Striking Instance of the Usefulness of Prophecy, Exemplified in the Case of John Earl of Rochester, Who Died at Woodstock-Park, July 26, 1680. Extracted from His Funeral Sermon, Preached by His Lordship's Chaplain, Robert Parsons, A.M.," *The Gospel Magazine, or Spiritual Library, Designed to Promote Scriptural Religion* 6 (May 1771): 227–230.[10]

19. *The Wonderful Extremes United in the Person of Christ. proposed as Brief Hints of Thought, and Materials of Meditation, for True Christians. to which are added Easy and Beautiful Demonstrations of the Immortality of the Soul. Extracted from Dr. Doddridge. The Foreknowledge of the Holy Spirit, a Glorious Evidence of his Divinity* (London: M. Lewis and J. Gurney, 1772).[11]

20. "Easy and Beautiful Demonstrations of the Existence of a God. Extracted from Dr. Doddridge, with some Additions," *The Gospel Magazine, or Spiritual Library, Designed to Promote Scriptural Religion* 7 (January 1772): 4–11.

21. "Deists Proved to Be Defective in Integrity and Common Sense: or Infidels, Convicted of the Utmost Folly, and the Most Detestable Dishonesty," *The Gospel Magazine, or Spiritual Library, Designed to Promote Scriptural Religion* 7 (March 1772): 103–106; (July 1772): 308–310.

22. "The Soul An Amazing Image of God," *The Gospel Magazine, or Spiritual Library, Designed to Promote Scriptural Religion* 7 (September 1772): 407–411; (October 1772): 455–456.

23. *A Modest Plea for Free Communion at the Lord's Table; Between True Believers of All Denominations* (N.p.: n.p., 1772).[12]

24. "The Insufficiency of Reason to Give Proper Discoveries Concerning God and His Infinite Perfections. The True Manner of Worshipping God. The Supreme Good of Man. The Perfect Rule of Morality. The Most Powerful Motives to Virtue and Religion. The Origin of Moral Evil. The Pardon of

---

[10] The first part is an excerpt from Parson's sermon and Ryland suffixes his own letter "to the Deists of the present day."

[11] Before being published together, these essays originally appeared in the December 1771 edition of *The Gospel Magazine, or Spiritual Library, Designed to Promote Scriptural Religion* 6 (1771): 502–506, 522–524, 526–528.

[12] Ryland wrote this under the pseudonym, "Pacificus."

Sin. The Refinement and Purification of the Soul. Support Under the Afflictions and Troubles of Life—And Consolations against the Stings and Terrors of Death—Evinced in a Series of Short Lectures," *The Gospel Magazine, or Spiritual Library, Designed to Promote Scriptural Religion* 8 (September 1773): 480–487.

25. *\*The Voice of God in His Threatnings; or the Infinite Terrors of Divine Justice, Against All Ranks and Orders of Wilful and Impenitent Sinners. Collected and Methodized Under Proper Heads* (post-1773).[13]
26. *A Contemplation on the Existence and Perfections of God, Drawn from the Several Parts of the Visible World, the Structure of the Body and the Wonderful Powers of the Soul; as an Image of the Wisdom, Power, and the Invisible and Immortal Nature of God* (London: Vallance and Simmons, 1774).
27. *A Contemplation on the Insufficiency of Reason, and the Necessity of Divine Revelation to Enable us to Attain Eternal Happiness, to which is Prefixed, The Character of an Honest Free-thinker* (London: Vallance and Simmons, 1775).
28. *\*A Contemplation on the Nature, Malignity, Guilt, and Madness of Pride* (post-1775).[14]
29. *\*A Contemplation on the Nature of Inspiration, with a Demonstration of the Reality thereof, in the sacred Writings of the Old and New Testament* (post-1775).[15]
30. *\*A Contemplation on the Real and Perfect Satisfaction of Christ* (pre-1776).[16]
31. *A Contemplation on the Nature and Evidences of the Divine Inspiration of the Holy Scriptures. With a Preface on the Nature of Rational and Divine Faith* (London: Thomas Dicey, 1776).
32. *A Farther Contemplation on the Nature and Evidences of the Divine Inspiration of the Holy Scriptures: Part II, with a Preface on the Nature, Malignity, Guilt, and Madness of Infidelity* (Northampton: Vallance and Simmons, 1776).
33. *\*Contemplations on the Sins, Vices, and Follies of Professors of Religion, and Careless Protestant Sinners of All Denominations: With the Opposite Graces*

---

[13] Noted as "shortly will be printed" in the 1767 and 1773 editions of *The Believer's Triumph in God's Promises*. It is unknown if this was ever published.

[14] It is noted as, "will be published in due time," at the beginning of *A Contemplation on the Insufficiency of Reason* (1775).

[15] It is noted as, "shortly will be published," at the end of *A Contemplation on the Insufficiency of Reason* (1775).

[16] It is noted as "published" in *A Contemplation on the Nature and Evidences of the Divine Inspiration of the Holy Scriptures* (1776). It is also noted as "published afresh" in *The Gospel Magazine* in 1771, 1772, and 1773.

and Virtues (post-1776).[17]

34. *The Beauty of Social Religion; or, the Nature and Glory of a Gospel Church. Represented in a Circular Letter from the Baptist Ministers and Messengers, Assembled at Oakham, in Rutlandshire, May 20, 21, 1777* (Northampton: T. Dicey, 1777).

35. *Contemplations on the Beauties of Creation and on all the Principal Truths and Blessings of the Glorious Gospel; with the Sins and Graces of Professing Christians* (London: Edward and Charles Dilly and T. Vallance, 1777).[18]

36. \*A *Contemplation on the Principal Rules for Understanding the Whole Book of the Revelations* (pre-1779).[19]

37. *The Overthrow of Popery Predicted. The Book of Revelation Explained* (1779, repr., London: Aylott and Jones, 1850).

38. \*A *Contemplation on Miracles, as a Glorious Evidence of the Divine Inspiration of the Holy Scriptures* (London: T. Dicey, 1779).[20]

39. *The Wise Student and Christian Preacher. A Sermon, Preached at Broad-Mead, August 28, 1780, being the day of the Annual Meeting of the Bristol Education Society* (Bristol: W. Pine, 1780).

40. \**Contemplations on a Special and Particular Providence; or a Demonstration That All Things in Heaven, Earth, and Hell, Must Needs Work for the Good of Every Person Who Fears and Loves God the Redeemer; with References to Select Books on Each Head* (post-1781).[21]

41. "A Demonstration of the Inspiration of the Scriptures" began in *The Protestant Magazine, or Christian Treasury* 1 (November 1781): 174–176; and continued in *The Protestant Magazine, or Christian Treasury* 2 (January 1782): 34–35.

42. "An Answer to the Questions on the Wisdom of God in Creation, and on

---

[17] It is noted as "preparing for the Press" at the conclusion of *A Farther Contemplation on the Nature and Evidences of the Divine Inspiration of the Holy Scriptures* (1776).

[18] This is volume one of his Contemplations series. Reprinted 1780. A second title page reads: *A Contemplation on the Existence and Perfections of God, Drawn from the Several Parts of the Visible World, to the Structure of the Human Body, and the Wonderful Powers of the Soul; as an Image of the Wisdom, Power, and the Invisible and Immortal Nature of God.*

[19] This title is mentioned in a short note in *The Baptist Magazine* 43 (1851): 35.

[20] This is volume two of his Contemplations series. With varying titles, it is noted as published in numerous works of Ryland. (e. g., *Contemplations on the Evidences of Inspiration, Arising from Miracles, Prophecies, and Their Fulfillment; the Noble and Beautiful Character of the Great Founder of Christianity; Rules for Understanding the Scriptures in General, and the Book of Revelations in Particular; the Noble and Sublime Character of God, Arising from His Natural Perfections* mentioned as "lately published" at the beginning of *Contemplations on the Divinity of Christ* [1782]).

[21] This book is noted as "going to the press, to be published by subscription," at the beginning of his *Dr. Cotton Mather's Student and Preacher* (1781). It is unknown if it was ever produced.

the Principles of the Gospel Applied to Christ," in *The Protestant Magazine, or Christian Treasury* 2 (July 1782): 259–264.

43. "Supplemental Thoughts to Awaken the Wise Zeal of Protestants to Promote and Propagate Their Religion," in *The Protestant Magazine, or Christian Treasury* 2 (April 1782): 141–147.
44. "A Striking Fact of the Conversion of a Lady in Scotland from Popery," *The Protestant Magazine, or Christian Treasury* 2 (November 1782): 427–431.
45. "A Demonstration of the Immortality of the Soul," began in the November edition of *The Protestant Magazine, or Christian Treasury* 2 (London: R. Denham, 1782): 401–406, 420, 465–466, 483–490; and continued in *The Protestant Magazine, or Christian Treasury* 3 (January 1783): 12–16, 22–25.
46. "The Awful Charge of Divine Justice Against Man on His First Revolt from God," *The Protestant Magazine, or Christian Treasury* 2 (December 1782): 441–447.[22]
47. "A View of the Riches of the Covenant of Grace, or Strong Cordials for True Christians, Arising from the Absolute Promises and Rich Privileges of the Gospel," in the Supplement to *The Protestant Magazine, or Christian Treasury* 2 (1782): 481–483.
48. *Contemplations on the Divinity of Christ, Evinced from His Names Jehovah, God, and Sovereign Lord; His Attributes and Actions; the Beauties of Creation, Providence, and Redemption; and the Acts of Worship Paid to Him in Scripture* (London: Thomas Dicey and Co., 1782).[23]
49. "The Ardent Pleadings of Divine Mercy in Behalf of Man, on His Fall from God into Misery," *The Protestant Magazine, or Christian Treasury* 3 (January 1783): 7–10.
50. "The Oath of God," *The Protestant Magazine, or Christian Treasury* 3 (January 1783): 10–11.
51. "Some Particulars Relative to the Life of the Good and Learned John Leusden, Doctor of Philosophy, and Professor of the Hebrew Language in the University of Utrecht 50 Years. Extracted from His Funeral Oration by Gerard de Vries, Delivered in the Great Theatre, Oct. 12, 1699," *The Protestant Magazine, or Christian Treasury* 3 (January 1783): 20–22.
52. "Socinians Proved to be Defective in Integrity and Common Sense, or the Disciples of Socinus Convicted of the Most Glaring Folly and the Most Detestable and Contemptible Dishonesty," *The Protestant Magazine, or Christian Treasury* 3 (January 1783): 31–35.
53. *A Sermon Occasioned by the Death of the Rev. Andrew Gifford, D.D., by John*

---

[22] This same title appears in *The New Spiritual Magazine; or Evangelical Treasury of Experimental Religion* vol. 3, no. 22 (1785): 596–600.

[23] This is volume three of his Contemplations series.

*Rippon Preached at Eagle Street; with An Address Delivered at His Interment, by the Rev. John Ryland, A.M.* 2nd ed. (London: T. Wilkins, 1784).[24]

54. "The Glory of the Church in the Latter Day," *The New Spiritual Magazine; or Evangelical Treasury of Experimental Religion* vol. 3, no. 21–30 (1785): 579–582, 621–624, 663–665, 701–702, 744–746, 778–780, 863, 906–908.[25]

55. "Table of Testimonies Brought over from the Old Testament to the New," *The New Spiritual Magazine; or Evangelical Treasury of Experimental Religion* vol. 3, no. 25 (1785): 702–708.

56. "Table of Testimonies Brought over from the Old Testament to the New, Yet Not Retaining the Same Words, Only the Same Meaning," *The New Spiritual Magazine; or Evangelical Treasury of Experimental Religion* vol. 3, no. 26 (1785): 746–750.

57. \**Views of the Wonderful Powers and Operations of Jesus* (London: R. Hindmarsh, 1785).[26]

58. *An Introduction to the Knowledge of the Holy Spirit, as a Divine Person in the Undivided Being of God, with a View of His Works of Creation, Inspiration and Miracles, Regeneration and Perseverance, and the Resurrection of the Dead, with the Worship Due to Him in the Churches of Christ* (London: Thomas Wilkins, 1786).[27]

59. *A View of the Corrupt Principles of Socinianism, Designed as an Introduction to Dr. John Owen on Divine Justice, and His Answer to Biddle* (pre-1787).[28]

60. *Contemplations on the Eternal and Immutable Justice of God, from the Latin Dissertations of Dr. Owen ... Designed as a Full Answer to the Essential Parts*

---

[24] Reprinted in 1790, 1834, 1849, and 1888.

[25] The whole volume is dedicated to John Ryland.

[26] Noted in the Wallis checklist.

[27] Ryland's name does not appear in the document, but an entry in *The Christian's Magazine* (January 1792, likely by William Newman [1773–1835]) confirms Ryland as the author. See *The Christian's Magazine* 3 (1792), 34.

This title appears to be the same piece or a version of *Contemplations on the Divinity of the Holy Spirit; the Beauties of Creation, and Providence. of Regeneration, Sanctification, or Vital Holiness; and Final Perseverance in Grace*. This was planned to be volume four in his Contemplations series. It is unknown whether it was written or published under this title. This title is proposed for subscription at the end of his *Contemplations on the Divinity of Christ* (1782). It is also proposed for subscription under this title at the end of his *A Sermon Occasioned by the Death of the Rev. Andrew Gifford, D.D.* (1784), with the comment that "the manuscript has been preparing for many years," but that there were not yet enough subscribers to merit a print run.

[28] This title is indicated as "just published, by the Rev. John Ryland, sen. of Northampton" at the end of the 1791 edition of Ryland's republication of Alleine's *The Voice of God in His Promises*. A second edition was published by John Eades in London in 1826. It is printed with William Huntington's commendatory preface, dated February 1787.

*of Socinianism* (London: W. Justins, 1787).
61. *Threatenings of Divine Justice against Particular Sins* (London: W. Justins, 1787).
62. *\*Demonstrating of Divine Justice. In Numbers. No. 1* (London: Symonds, 1790).
63. *A Body of Divinity in Miniature, Designed for the Use of the Youth of Great Britain and France* (London: T. Chapman, 1790).[29]
64. *The Character of the Rev. James Hervey, M.A., Late Rector of Weston-Flavel, in Northamptonshire. Considered, As a Man of Genius and a Preacher—As a Philosopher and Christian United—As a Regenerate Man—As a Man Endowed with Dignity and Prerogatives of a Christian—As a Man of Science and Virtue—As a Divine or a Very Eminent Master in the Doctrines and Duties of the Christian Religion. With Sixty-Five of His Original Letters, to the Author of This Life; and His Real Likeness on a Copper Plate* (London: W. Justins and R. Thomson, 1790).[30]
65. *A Picture of Popery; or, A Clear View of the Corrupt Principles of the Papists: Being The Popish Creed, Drawn from Their Own Books* (London: W. Hepinstal, 1791).[31]
66. *An Address to the Ingenuous Youth of Great Britain. Together with a Body of Divinity in Miniature. To Which Is Subjoined a Plan of Education, Adapted to the Use of Schools, and Which Has Been Carried into Execution During a Course of Near Fifty Years* (London: H. D. Symonds, 1792).[32]
67. *Select Essays on the Moral Virtues, and on Genius, Science, and Taste, Interspersed with Striking Facts. Being the Author's Last Present to the Public, in the Seventieth Year of His Age* (London: H. D. Symonds, 1792).[33]
68. *Evidences that the Christian Religion is of God* (London: W. Smith, 1798).[34]

---

[29] Reprinted in 1792 and 1814.

[30] Reprinted in 1791.

[31] Ryland's essay is prefixed to *Colloquia Mensalia; or the Familiar Discourses of Dr. Martin Luther at His Table, Which in His Lifetime He Held with Divers Learned Men.* trans. by Henry Bell (London: W. Hepinstal, 1791).

[32] Reprinted in 1802, 1814. A note says the initial address was first published in 1768, and the *Plan of Education* was first published in 1766.

[33] Selections of his *Striking Facts* were excerpted and printed in *The Evangelical Museum or Christian's Pocket Book. for the Year 1792* (London: H. D. Symonds, 1792), and again in *The Evangelical Museum or Christian's Pocket Book. for the Year 1793* (London: H. D. Symonds, 1793).

[34] Reprinted as *Brief Evidences of the Christian Religion.* (London: J. F. Winks and G. Wightman, 1840). Starr notes a fourth edition in 1806.

69. "Reflections" (date unknown).³⁵
70. "The Palace of Science, and the Temple of Contemplation and Devotion: A Fragment by the Late Rev. Mr. Ryland," *The Baptist Magazine* 11 (1819): 6–10.

*Ryland's Scientific and Educational Works*³⁶
1. \**The Elements of Geography, with Seven Copper-Plates* (London: J. and W. Oliver, 1763).³⁷
2. \**Astronomy for School Boys* (1766).³⁸
3. \**A Plan of Education Attempted at Northampton* (London: T. and J. W. Pasham, 1766).³⁹
4. \**English Grammar* (1767).⁴⁰
5. *An Essay on the Dignity and Usefulness of Human Learning* (London, 1769).
6. \**A Compendium of the Whole Greek Testament: Exhibiting, in the Clearest Point of View, Every Primitive Word in that Sacred Book* (post-1770).⁴¹
7. \**Lectures on the Most Beautiful and Sublime Parts of the Poetical and Devotional Writings of the Hebrew Prophets, &c. Read in the University of Oxford, by Robert Lowth, D.D. Late Professor of Poetry, and Now Bishop of Oxford* (post-1770).⁴²
8. *An Essay on the Advancement of Learning, In various Modes of Recreation* (1772).⁴³

---

³⁵ This is an anonymous hymn in the October edition of *The Evangelical Magazine for 1798* (London: T. Chapman, 1798), 439. Thomas Wright attributes this hymn to John Collett Ryland and notes that it was the only hymn that Ryland wrote (see Thomas Wright, *Augustus M. Toplady and Contemporary Hymn-Writers* [London: Farncombe & Son, 1911], 273).

³⁶ I have not included his collections of cards in this list of publications. For his educational subjects, he commissioned to be printed something like double-sided flash cards as a memory device for his students (e. g. see the list at the end of *An Easy Introduction to Mechanics, Geometry, Plane Trigonometry, Measuring Heights and Distances, Optics, Astronomy* [1768]).

³⁷ Noted as "published" in *A Contemplation on the Nature and Evidences of the Divine Inspiration of the Holy Scriptures* (1776).

³⁸ Noted in the Wallis checklist.

³⁹ Republished in *An Address to the Ingenuous Youth of Great Britain* (1792).

⁴⁰ Noted in the Starr bibliography.

⁴¹ Advertised at the end of *The Scheme of Infidelity Ruined For Ever* (1770) but it is unknown if it was ever produced.

⁴² This work is noted to be translated from Latin by Hugh Walford (at Ryland's request) and revised by Ryland and his friend, William Hextal. It is advertised, along with a brief outline of the work, at the end of *The Scheme of Infidelity Ruined For Ever* (1770) but it is unknown if it was ever produced.

⁴³ Prefixed to his *An Easy and Pleasant Introduction to Sir Isaac Newton's Philosophy* (1772), but this essay

9. \*An Easy and Pleasant Compendium of almost the whole Hebrew Bible. Containing and Select Verses, a Quarter Part of the Book of Psalms, divided into LVI. Short Lessons of Ten Verses each, including near 1200 Hebrew Roots of principal and frequent Use, with an English Translation of each Root (post-1772).[44]
10. \*A Compendium of the Greek Testament. Containing in Near Two Thousand Select Verses, a Quarter Part of that Sacred Book, Including Near Five Thousand Primitive Words, with an English Translation of Each Word (post-1772).[45]
11. \*An Easy System of Geography, in Familiar Latin (pre-1776).[46]
12. \*Ancient History, in Two Sets of Cards; the First, from the Creation to the Battle of Marathon; the Second Set, from the Battle of Marathon to the Birth of Christ (pre-1776).
13. \*A Most Easy Introduction to the Science of Optics; or, The Doctrine of Light and Colours. Engraved on Copper-Plates (pre-1776).
14. \*Easy and Familiar French and English Conversations, for Boys and Girls at Boarding-Schools, Suited to Morning, Noon, and Evening; and for Breakfast, Dinner, and Supper (pre-1776).
15. \*Patterns of the Regular Latin Verbs in Four Conjugations. A Broad Sheet (pre-1776).
16. \*Cellarius's Initiating Exercises, with Many Easy Latin Phrases and Dialogues (pre-1776).
17. \*A Clear View of the Patterns of Twenty-Five Greek Nouns—the Patterns of the Greek Adjectives, Pronouns, and Verbs. Four Large Sheets (pre-1776).
18. \*An Easy Introduction to the Hebrew Language: With an Analysis of the Whole First Chapter of Genesis, Tracing Out Every Word to Its Root; With Rules for Learning Hebrew: And a Collection of Select Hebrew Books (pre-1776).
19. The Preceptor, or Counsellor of Human Life; for the use of the British Youth (London, 1776).[47]

---

also circulated independently.

[44] Advertised in *The Scheme of Infidelity Ruined Forever* (1770), and noted as, "shortly will be published," at the end of *An Easy and Pleasant Introduction to Sir Isaac Newton's Philosophy* (1772).

[45] Noted as, "shortly will be published," at the end of *An Easy Introduction to Mechanics, Geometry, Plane Trigonometry, Measuring Heights and Distances, Optics, Astronomy* (1768) and *An Easy and Pleasant Introduction to Sir Isaac Newton's Philosophy* (1772).

[46] Items 11–18 are noted as "published" in *A Contemplation on the Nature and Evidences of the Divine Inspiration of the Holy Scriptures* (1776).

[47] This volume was compiled by Ryland, with his own preface, introduction, and various chapters. This was also published under the alternative title *The Preceptor, or General Repository of Useful Information, Very*

20. *A Key to the Greek Oration of Demosthenes For the Crown: Exhibiting in the clearest Point of View, every Primitive Word in the first Part of the Oration. with An English Translation of each Root. Designed For the Youth at Schools, and to assist those Young Persons of Taste, who would gladly recover the Knowledge of the Greek they had attained at School* (post-1776).[48]
21. *An Introduction to Homer's Iliad* (post-1776).
22. *The General Plutarch; or Select Lives of Illustrious Men, In Different Ages and Nations* (post-1776).[49]
23. *A Key to the Greek New Testament: exhibiting in the Clearest Point of View Every Primitive Word in that Sacred Book: with an English Translation of each Root* (London: George Keith and Edward and Charles Dilly, 1777).
24. *A Grammar and Key to the Greek New Testament in English* (1777).[50]
25. *An English and Greek Grammar, Designed as an Introduction to a Key to the Greek New Testament* (London: G. Keith and E. and C. Dilly, 1777).[51]
26. *The Life and Character of Alfred the Great. Drawn from the More Ample View of Him in the First Volume Folio of the Biographia Britannica, with Other Authors* (London: Charles Dilly and John Stockdale, 1784).[52]
27. *Geographical and Astronomical Definitions, so far as They Relate to the Use of the Globes* (Northampton: T. Dicey, 1785).[53]
28. *The Corner Stone of the British Constitution, or the Golden Passage in the Great Charter of England Called Magna Charta, or the Charter of British Liberties* (London: W. Justins, 1789).[54]
29. *A Tribute of Honor to the Great and Good Men in France; Particularly the Marquis de la Fayette, Mr. Nekar, and the Most Worthy of All Mayors—The Mayor of Paris; with the President of the National Assembly* (London: T. Chapman, 1790).

---

*Necessary for the Various Ages and Different Departments of Life* (London: Dilly, 1775).

[48] Items 20–21 are noted as, "ready for the press," at the end of *The Preceptor* (1776). But it is unknown if they were ever published.

[49] Noted as, "speedily will be published," at the end of *The Preceptor* (1776). But it is unknown if it was ever published.

[50] Noted as, "just published," at the beginning of *Contemplations on the Beauties of Creation* (1777).

[51] Noted in the Wallis checklist and Starr bibliography.

[52] This also appeared in parts in *The Protestant Magazine, or Christian Treasury* 2 (September–December 1782).

[53] Noted in the Wallis checklist.

[54] Noted as "just published" at the end of *A Body of Divinity in Miniature* (1790). Ryland's authorship is assumed.

*Ryland's Prefaces, Introductions, Recommendations, and Republications*
1. Ryland's introductory memoir of Joseph Alleine (1634–1668) and the republication of *The Voice of God in His Promises; or, Strong Consolation for True Christians. Being the Substance and Spirit of the Covenant of Grace. Extracted from the Writings of Rev. Mr. Joseph Alleine, Late Minister of the Gospel at Taunton, in Somersetshire* (London: T. and J. W. Pasham, 1766).[55]
2. Ryland's preface for, and the republication of, *The Believer's Triumph in God's Promises; and the various Conflicts and Glorious Conquests of Faith over Unbelief: being an Appendix to the Voice of God in His Promises. by the Reverend Mr. Joseph Alleine, Late Minister of the Gospel at Taunton in Somersetshire* (London: T. and J. W. Pasham, 1767).[56]
3. *The Easiest Introduction to Dr. Lowth's English Grammar, Designed for the Use of Children under Ten Years of Age, To lead them into a Knowledge of the First Principles of the English Language. By the Rev. John Ash, of Pershore in Worcestershire* (London: E. and C. Dilly, 1768).[57]
4. *The Private Tutor to Sententiae Pueriles, Reduced to the Natural Order of Construction with a Close English Version, and Divided into Three Lessons for Every Day in the Week, Till the Whole Be Finished; Having Also Subjoined Tables Containing the Variations of the Declinable Parts of Speech* (London: E. and C. Dilly, 1769).[58]
5. *Easy and Pleasant Latin Conversations; or, One Hundred and Forty-four Dialogues on Common Subjects, Morals, and the First Part of the Roman History. By Dr. Lange, of Hall, in Saxony* (London: Edward and Charles Dilly, 1769).[59]
6. *\*The Malignity and Misery of Lewdness, … and the Dignity and Happiness of Chastity Demonstrated* (London, 1769).[60]
7. *Grammar and Pleasure United; or, An Easy Introduction to the English and Latin Languages in Verse* (London: E. and C. Dilly, 1770).[61]

---

[55] Reprinted in 1768 and 1791.

[56] Reprinted in 1773 and 1789.

[57] Ryland edited "A New Edition, Improved" of a work by John Ash (1724–1779), adding his own introduction and a lengthy appendix.

[58] Ryland edited and expanded a portion of John Stirling's (d. 1777) *The Private Tutor to the British Youth* (London, 1763), which was dedicated to Ryland.

[59] Ryland edited Johann Joachim Lange's (1670–1744) work and affixed an introduction and an extended preface, *On the Dignity and Privileges of Human Learning*.

[60] Ryland republished this work by Matthew Henry (1662–1714) for the use of his school. Noted in the Wallis checklist.

[61] Ryland republished this work by Jenkin-Thomas Phillips.

8. *An Easy and Pleasant Introduction to Sir Isaac Newton's Philosophy: Containing the First Principles of Mechanics, Trigonometry, Optics, and Astronomy. By a Fellow of the Royal Society. With an Essay on the Advancement of Learning, in Various Modes of Recreation*, 2nd edition (London: Edward and Charles Dilly, 1772).62
9. *\*A Compendium of Natural Philosophy, Containing Mechanics, Hydrostatics, Pneumatics, Optics and Astronomy. By John Horsley, A.M. Adapted to a Course of Experiments Performed in Glasgow* (post-1772).63
10. Ryland's recommendation prefixed to Benjamin Keach's (1640–1704) *Tropologia: A Key to Open Scripture Metaphors, in Four Books. To which are prefixed Arguments to prove the Divine Authority of the Holy Scriptures* (London: J. W. Pasham, 1779).
11. Ryland's preface to his republication of *The Excellency of Christ. A Sermon, preached at Northampton, in New England, In the Time of the wonderful Work of Grace there, in the Year 1738. By the late President Jonathan Edwards* (Northampton: T. Dicey, 1780).
12. Ryland's "recommendatory preface" for *The Whole Works Of that Eminent Servant of Christ, the late Reverend and much Esteemed Mr. John Bunyan, Formerly Minister of the Gospel, and Pastor of a Congregation at Bedford; Including the Whole of his Pieces, Sermons, Discourses, Tracts, and Other Writings, on various Divine Subjects* (London: Alex Hogg, 1780).
13. Benjamin Bennet, *A View to the Whole System of Popery* (London: C. Dilly, 1781).64
14. Ryland's preface for *Dr. Cotton Mather's Student and Preacher. Intituled, Manuductio ad Ministerium; or, Directions for a Candidate of the Ministry* (London: Charles Dilly, 1781).65
15. Ryland's recommendation for John Bunyan's (1628–1688) *A True Relation of the Holy War, Made by King Shaddai Upon Diabolus, for the Regaining of the Metropolis of the World: or, the Losing and Taking Again of the Town of*

---

⁶² This book was authored by James Ferguson (1710–1776), according to Ryland, *Contemplations on the Divinity of Christ* (1782), viii. It is a republication of Ryland's *An Easy Introduction to Mechanics, Geometry, Plane Trigonometry, Measuring Heights and Distances, Optics, Astronomy. to Which is Prefixed an Essay on the Advancement of Learning by Various Modes of Recreation* (London: Edward and Charles Dilly, 1768) with the added appendix of lectures by Ferguson entitled, *Experimental Philosophy for School-Boys: or, an Appendix to the Introduction to the Newtonian Philosophy*.

⁶³ Noted as "shortly will be published," at the beginning of *An Easy and Pleasant Introduction to Sir Isaac Newton's Philosophy* (1772).

⁶⁴ This volume is noted as "republished by the Rev. Mr. Ryland," *The Protestant Magazine, or Christian Treasury* 2 (1782), 456. The advertisement at the beginning of the Bennet treatise appears to be from Ryland.

⁶⁵ A lengthy appendix of "Notes and Observations" from Ryland appears at the end. A "revised and corrected" edition of this work was published in 1789 by "a lover of the gospel."

*Mansoul* (London: Alex Hogg, 1784).
16. Ryland's recommendation for *A New Edition. Fox's Book of Martyrs, Containing Copious and Authentic Accounts of the Lives, Sufferings and Deaths of the Protestant Martyrs in the Reign of Queen Mary the First* (London: Alex Hogg, 1785?).66
17. Ryland's preface for *The Elements of Geography, short and plain. Designed as an easy Introduction to the System of Geography, in Verse, by Robert Davidson. Esq. Designed for the use of Schools. With or Without Seven Copper Plates* (London: T. Wilkins, 1788).
18. Ryland revised and affixed his "recommendatory preface" to *Christus in Corde: or, the Mystical Union Between Christ and Believers, Considered in Its Resemblances, Bonds, Seals, Privileges, and Marks. By Edward Polhill, of Burwash, in Sussex, Esq.* (London: R. Thomson and J. Higham, 1788).
19. Ryland's translation from the Latin of John Owen's, *A Dissertation on Divine Justice: or, The Claims of Vindicatory Justice Asserted* (London: L. J. Higham and J. Murgatroyd, 1790).67
20. Ryland's preface to Maria de Fleury's (fl. 1773–1791) *Divine Poems and Essays on Various Subjects* (London, 1791).
21. *\*An Abridgement of the Three Vols. of Alleine's Vindicia Pietatis* (post-1791).68
22. Ryland's recommendation for Francis Quarles, *Emblems, Divine and Moral* (Bristol: Joseph Lansdown and John Mills, 1808).

---

[66] Reprinted in 1795(?). Ryland states in his graveside sermon for Andrew Gifford (1784) that the book is "now publishing."

[67] Ryland appears to have translated and co-authored the preface with John Stafford and Robert Simpson.

[68] Noted as "shortly will be published" in the 1791 edition of *The Voice of God in His Promises* (1791).

# "To promote the love of Christ": Joseph Priestley, Andrew Fuller, and the deity of Christ as the basis for Christian morality

Andrew B. Lawson

Andrew B. Lawson (ThM, The Southern Baptist Theological Seminary) is a doctoral student in Church History at The Southern Baptist Theological Seminary, Louisville, KY.

---

In an apologetic work written in 1799, Andrew Fuller (1754–1815) wrote a moving story about the self-sacrificing love of a noble prince. Foreign enemies had convinced members of the nation's army to commit treason against his father, the king. The rebels had failed and been captured, but the king was still distraught. His heart was inclined to show mercy, but he knew that would not be just. Excusing treason and rebellion would lead to the ruin of his realm—there must be a price paid. A mediator needed to be found, someone who could both satisfy the demands of justice and offer mercy to the conspirators for his own sake. This person needed to be innocent and above reproach of the crime committed, high in the esteem of both the king and the country, filled with compassion for the guilty, and with a close relation to them. The king's beloved son, the general of all his armies, took him aside and volunteered to act as substitute and mediator. He was a soldier like the accused, his heart was filled with compassion for them, and nobody could question his dignity or authority. The king and his son shared the same mind, and on the appointed day of judgment the prince endured the shameful beatings that the traitors ought to have suffered. The whole court was struck with awe and love for this prince, who was ready "to suffer in the place of rebels … beyond all that could have been asked or thought."[1] Later, hearing of how the prince had taken the punishment due to them, several of the rebels left their disaffected fellows and repented of their treason. They were filled with admiration for the prince who had saved them, expressing that "the dignity of his character, together with his surprising condescension and goodness, impresses us more than anything else, and fills our hearts with penitence, confidence, and love."[2] The mediation of the prince had won them over.

In this extended parable, Fuller disclosed why Christians who believed in the atonement of Christ on the cross for the forgiveness of sins ought to love him most of all people everywhere. In his day various heterodox religious sects such as the Deists and Socinians were arguing that genuine love for Christ did not require belief in substitutionary atonement or his divine nature.[3] Fuller's most renowned opponent on this issue was Joseph Priestley (1733–1804), a Socinian who professed to hold the most exalted love for Christ while denying his divine nature and the necessity for atonement as understood by Calvinists like Andrew Fuller. Priestley was the most able proponent of his position, a man who commanded respect for his intelligence, high moral character, and stated reverence for the scriptures. A conflux of social and political events around the end of the eighteenth century set Fuller and Priestley at odds with one another, which led to Fuller's *Calvinistic and Socinian Systems Examined*, in which he sought to prove that Christians who held to orthodox understandings of Christ's nature and work on the Cross were under the greatest of compulsions to love Christ and follow his blessed example. Socinians such as Priestley did not have the same foundation for either affection towards Christ or "vital and practical religion" as did orthodox Christians.[4]

---

[1] Andrew Fuller, *The Gospel Its Own Witness; Or, The Holy Nature and Divine Harmony of the Christian Religion Contrasted with the Immorality and Absurdity of Deism. Part II. The Harmon of the Christian Religion Considered as an Evidence of its Divinity*, in *The Complete Works of the Rev. Andrew Fuller* (Harrisonburg, VA: Sprinkle Publications, 1988), 2:77.

[2] Fuller, *The Gospel Its Own Witness*, 2:79.

[3] Fuller preferred to describe this sect as Socinians, rather than Unitarians, their preferred term for themselves. He believed that granting them the title Unitarian was conceding that orthodox Trinitarians did not accept the unity of the godhead, thus conceding the debate. See Andrew Fuller, *The Calvinistic and Socinian Systems Examined and Compared as to Their Moral Tendency, in a Series of Letters, addressed to the Friends of Vital and Practical Religion, to which is added a Postscript, Establishing the Principle of the Work, Against the Exceptions of Dr. Toulmin, Mr. Belsham, Etc.*, in *The Complete Works of the Rev. Andrew Fuller*, 2:110–111.

[4] This phrase is alluded too from the extended subtitle of Fuller, *Calvinistic and Socinian Systems Examined*, 2:108.

*Joseph Priestley and "Rational Religion"*

Joseph Priestley was one of the most brilliant and eclectic Englishmen of the eighteenth century. He was born into a moderately wealthy family of dissenters in Yorkshire in 1733. Dissenters were not permitted to attend English universities, and Priestley was educated at the dissenting academy in Northamptonshire. He showed unusual skill in many subjects, including philosophy, languages, and science, but became most renowned for his religious opinions. By the time he was ordained as a dissenting minister in 1762, Priestley was a convinced Arian—believing Jesus was a creature instead of the creator, and his religious journey was not yet over.

Priestley was called to the pastorate of Mill Hill Chapel in 1767, a dissenting congregation with a history of regression away from the Calvinist views of their heritage. Mill Hill had been organized as an orthodox Presbyterian gathering after Charles II issued his Declaration of Indulgence in 1672 and maintained its Calvinism till the pastorate of Joseph Cappe from 1730 to 1748. Cappe was an orthodox Trinitarian but rejected Calvinism in favor of an Arminian soteriology.[5] His successor Thomas Walker pastored Mill Hill from 1748 to 1763. Walker moved further from traditional doctrine than Cappe had. He promoted Arianism and doubted the doctrine of substitutionary atonement. By the time Priestley became the minister at Mill Hill in 1767 the Calvinist members of the congregation had all departed the fellowship to form their own orthodox gatherings.[6] The transition of Mill Hill Chapel from orthodox Presbyterianism into Arminianism and then Arianism can serve as a microcosm of the widespread departure of English Presbyterianism from the doctrine established in the Westminster Confession of Faith in 1646.[7]

By 1772, Priestley had rejected Arianism—which still taught that Christ ought to be prayed too and worshipped—and become a full-fledged Socinian. He was not at all shy about his new beliefs. He taught on the merits of Socinianism in a series of classes at Mill Hill and dispersed his arguments in tracts and pamphlets across Leeds.[8] Priestley would later condense and refine his position and publish it in two volumes as the *Institutes of Natural and Revealed Religion*.[9] Priestley no longer believed that Jesus Christ was the proper recipient

---

[5] Robert E. Schofield, *The Enlightenment of Joseph Priestley: A Study of His Life and Work from 1733 to 1773* (University Park, PA: The Pennsylvania State University Press, 1997), 168.

[6] Anne Holt, *A Life of Joseph Priestley* (Westport, CT: Greenwood Press, 1970), 42–43.

[7] James C. Spalding, "The Demise of English Presbyterianism: 1660–1760," *Church History* 28, no. 1 (March 1959): 63–83.

[8] Schofield, *The Enlightenment of Joseph Priestley*, 172–173.

[9] Joseph Priestley, *Institutes of Natural and Revealed Religion in Two Volumes, to Which is Prefixed, an Essay on the best Method of Communicating Religious Knowledge to the Members of Christian Societies*

of divine worship. He argued in works such as *An History of Early Opinions Concerning Jesus Christ* and *History of the Corruptions of Christianity* that the Trinity was a gnostic interpolation into the simple faith in one God taught by Jesus and the first generation of his followers.[10] Priestley was happy to identify Jesus Christ in these works as the messiah of God's people and the mediator between God and man, but he did not understand these terms in the same way as a Trinitarian Christian. Jesus of Nazareth was unique because of his special calling and adoption by God, the ultimate prophet, teacher, and moral example for humanity, but certainly not divine. By 1786, Priestley had even abandoned the doctrine of the virgin birth, which had been retained by other Socinians.[11]

Priestley did not shy away from the implications of his denial of Jesus' divinity, nor was he willing to hold his views personally without seeking to spread them. He was convinced that his position was taught in the Bible and ought to be received by all Christians, lest they fall into the dangerous error of worshipping a man as God. He was a zealous and urgent evangelist for his views—in his Socinian apologetic *An Appeal to the Serious and Candid Professors of Christianity* (1784), he warned orthodox believers that the doctrine of the Trinity turned them into tri-theists, who are "guilty of a breach of the first and most important of all the commandments, which says expressly, 'Thou shalt have no other Gods before me.'"[12] Protestants who worshipped Jesus Christ were just as guilty of idolatry as superstitious Romans Catholics who "bowed down to, and worshipped, the work of their own hands."[13]

*Rational religion and morality*

Priestley had great ambitions for the future of Mill Hill as its pastor. He was not content to oversee a respectable, rational congregation untroubled by religious excesses. Rather, he was convinced that the tenets of Socinianism were

(London, 1794).

[10] Joseph Priestley, *An History of Early Opinions Concerning Jesus Christ, Compiled from Original Writers; Proving that the Christian Church was at First Unitarian* (Birmingham: Pearson and Rollason, 1790); item, *A History of the Corruptions of Christianity: To Which Are Appended Considerations in Evidence that the Apostolic and Primitive Church was Unitarian, Extracted from Priestley's Replies to Bishop Horsley, the Bench of Bishops, and Others* (London: The British and Foreign Unitarian Association, 1871).

[11] Holt, *Life of Joseph Priestley*, 138.

[12] Joseph Priestley, *An Appeal to the Serious and Candid Professors of Christianity. On the Following Subjects. I. The Use of Reason in Matters of Religion. II. The Power of Man to Do the Will of God. III. Original Sin. IV. Election and Reprobation. V. The Divinity of Christ, and VI. Atonement for Sin by the Death of Christ. By Joseph Priestly [sic], L.L.D. F.R.S. and a lover of the Gospel. To Which Are Added, a Concise History of the Rise of Those Doctrines: and the Triumph of the Truth; Being an Account of the Trial of Mr. E. Elwall, for heresy and blasphemy, at Stafford Assizes* (Philadelphia: Robert Bell, 1784), 13.

[13] Priestley, *Appeal to the Serious and Candid Professors of Christianity*, 16.

better suited than Christian orthodoxy to promote moral disciplines and was determined to prove it, especially among the young people of the congregation. Priestley believed that contemporary young people were not likely to be swayed by traditional Christianity, and he feared that rejecting faith would lead them to immoral and unprofitable lives. Rational Christianity would allow the new, more sophisticated generation to zealously embrace Christian morality by avoiding the stumbling blocks of superstitious corruptions such as the deity of Christ.

Priestley was dissatisfied with the moral discipline of the Mill Hall chapel and the Socinian movement in general. He lamented that the ministry of too many dissenter pastors was little more than "haranguing them once a week" with no real moral teaching.[14] He sought to correct this defect with an appeal to the youth of the congregation in his *A Catechism for Children and Young Persons*, published in 1768 one year after he began his pastorate at Mill Hill.[15] Priestley believed that teaching a child on "the idea of God, of his duty, and of a future state" would impart "ideas as will be of some use to him at present, but of much more as he grows up."[16] Teaching children "a reverence for religion" and "its general dictates" at a young age "when the mind is tender, and apt to receive impressions, will lay a foundation for the principle of conscience … and operate as a real restraint upon vice and immorality as long as a person lives."[17] Priestley had earlier dedicated his *Institutes* to his "young friends" at Mill Hill, and his *Catechism* continued his determination to win the minds of the youth to a morally strict and pious form of rational Christianity.[18]

Fathers also had a key duty in the religion of their families. Priestley knew of the Dissenting tradition of pious home worship and was distressed that family devotions did not seem to be a priority in his congregation. He wrote *A Serious Address to Masters of Families* in 1769, as another part of his effort to reform Mill Hill chapel into the devout, rational Christian community he envisioned as the future of the faith.[19] He summarized his campaign for renewed moral vigor with the treatise *A Free Address to Protestant Dissenters*, in which he both urged renewed zeal for rational Christianity and blamed "the gross corruptions" that "have been introduced into this most excellent scheme of religion" for stifling the piety of men and women who would otherwise be good Chris-

---

[14] Holt, *Life of Joseph Priestley*, 45.

[15] Joseph Priestley, *A Catechism for Children and Young Persons* (London: J. Johnson, 1768).

[16] Priestley, *Catechism for Children*, v.

[17] Priestley, *Catechism for Children*, vi.

[18] Priestley, *Institutes of Natural and Revealed Religion*, 2.

[19] Schofield, *Enlightenment of Joseph Priestley*, 189.

tians.[20] Priestley both envied the devotion of previous generations of dissenters and blamed them for holding to doctrine that in his day was killing the faith of rational men and women in Britain. Foremost among those doctrinal corruptions in Priestley's mind was the deity of Christ and the worship of him as God.

Priestley's emphasis on moral discipline was inseparable from his affection for Christ and the example he set for all Christians with his morality and obedience to God. Christ's life was our divinely commissioned model and his resurrection by God assured us of hope of eternal life for the righteous.[21] However, he was certainly not the Son of God, the divine second person of the Trinity. In fact, Priestley argued vociferously that such a thought would have been shocking to Christ, who saw himself as the humble servant of the one God. Prayer to Christ was therefore idolatry, a point that Priestley expanded upon at length in the third section of his *An History of Early Opinions Concerning Jesus Christ*. Priestley argued that Jesus Christ had always prayed only to God the Father, and "with as much humility and resignation as the most dependent being in the universe could possibly do."[22] Christ had directed his disciples to address God the Father in the Lord's Prayer, and called them his brethren, or fellow men.[23]

After quoting extensively from prayers offered exclusively to God the Father in the New Testament and among the early church fathers, Priestley concluded that "we have no authority to pray to any other than that one God, to whom Christ himself prayed in his affliction."[24] Rejecting prayer to Christ was a key part of Priestley's campaign for a rational and morally disciplined Socinianism. If Christ was only a man, then prayer directed to him was an idolatrous superstition, one of the corruptions introduced into Christianity that had cooled the faith and moral fervor of the people. Priestley genuinely believed that if these corruptions would be excised from the Christian religion, then skeptics and the disillusioned would once again find the purified faith morally compelling.

*Andrew Fuller and the defense of Trinitarianism*
English Particular Baptist Andrew Fuller is largely remembered today for his revitalization of evangelism among Calvinistic Baptists and his role in the formation of the Baptist Missionary Society. Fuller became so connected with

---

[20] Joseph Priestley, *A Free Address to Protestant Dissenters, As Such* (Birmingham: Pearson and Rollason, 1788), 3.

[21] Schofield, *Enlightenment of Joseph Priestley*, 196.

[22] Priestley, *History of Early Opinions*, 36.

[23] Priestley, *History of Early Opinions*, 36–37.

[24] Priestley, *History of Early Opinions*, 45–46.

these campaigns that his position on them became known as "Fullerism" within his own lifetime. His apologetic works against Socinianism, though also greatly appreciated in his own time, have not retained the same level of influence. For example, in Peter Morden's recent biography, Fuller's controversial works on the Trinity are not covered and Joseph Priestley is never mentioned.[25]

Priestley and Fuller were of two different generations. Most of Priestley's theological works were written while Fuller was still either a teenager or an obscure young pastor thoroughly occupied with his duties. Fuller had wrestled with and rejected Arianism soon after his conversion.[26] He had been raised and converted within the Particular Baptist tradition, which by and large was a stronghold of confessional Trinitarianism among English dissenters. Fuller's treatment of Trinitarianism in his own personal confession presented to the Kettering congregation is orthodox and brief. He affirmed that "though God is one, yet he is also three—the Father, the Son, and the Holy Spirit. The idea which I think the Scriptures give us of each of the sacred three is that of person. I believe the Son to be truly and equally God, equal with the Father and the Holy Spirit. Everything I see in this sacred mystery appears to me above reason, but nothing contrary to it."[27] Fuller's definition is noteworthy in that he derives his belief in the Trinity from the scriptures and specifically excludes any waffling on the equal divinity of Jesus Christ with the Father, the very point of weakness among so many English dissenters outside the Particular Baptist tradition in the eighteenth century.

What provoked Andrew Fuller to confront Priestley's Socinianism? Fuller wrote *The Calvinistic and Socinian Systems Examined and Compared* in the aftermath of political and social turmoil that had culminated in a series of riots in Birmingham in 1791. Priestley and his friends had decided to hold a provocative celebration of the second anniversary of the storming of the Bastille in France on July 14. Popular opinion had already turned strongly against the French Revolution by this time, and on the set date a violent, pro-monarchist mob rampaged through his property and threatened his life.[28] In his preface to *Calvinistic and Socinian Systems Examined*, Fuller condemned the rioting as "detestable," and that his "regard, for justice and humanity made him feel

---

[25] Peter J. Morden, *The Life and Thought of Andrew Fuller (1754–1815)* (Crownhill, Devon: Paternoster, 2015).

[26] Michael A.G. Haykin, "'To Devote Ourselves to the Blessed Trinity': Andrew Fuller and the Defense of 'Trinitarian Communities,'" *Southern Baptist Journal of Theology* 17, no. 2 (2013): 7–8.

[27] Michael A.G. Haykin, *Reading Andrew Fuller* (Peterborough, ON: H&E, 2020), 8.

[28] R.E.W. Maddison, and Francis R. Madison, "Joseph Priestley and the Birmingham Riots," *Notes and Records of the Royal Society of London* 12, no. 1 (1956): 98–99.

much, on that occasion, for Dr. Priestley, and others who suffered with him."[29] The home of Fuller's own friend Samuel Pearce (1766–1799), a fellow Particular Baptist minister, had been ransacked during the rioting while Pearce was absent.

The rioters in Birmingham did not seem to be able to distinguish between orthodox dissenters and Socinians, an outcome Fuller feared not because he wished violence against his theological opponents but because he was apprehensive that all English dissenters were being labeled anti-trinitarian heretics and political troublemakers in the popular imagination. The years prior to the outbreak of violence had brought both orthodox and heterodox dissenters together in a political campaign against the Corporation and Test Acts.[30] English society discriminated against anyone who was not a faithful member of the Church of England and did not distinguish between Trinitarians and Socinians. Dissenters of all theological persuasions had denounced these laws as unjust and had launched a serious campaign for their repeal. Though Fuller had supported this effort, he was concerned that consequently the theological differences between dissenters were being minimized in the public mind. His fear was validated as first Anglican clergyman began to accuse all dissenters of holding loosely to trinitarianism and then violent mobs burned the property of Baptists and Socinians alike to cries of "Church and King!"[31]

Contrasting orthodox dissenters and Socinians such as Priestley was a key reason Fuller undertook to write *The Calvinistic and Socinian Systems Examined*. Another reason is presented in the extended title, *As To Their Moral Tendency*. Priestley's entire program revolved around reintroducing strict moralism into Christianity, and he blamed Trinitarians for its decline. The "corruptions" of the simple faith in one God were to blame. In *Calvinistic and Socinian Systems Examined*, Fuller directly confronted this argument, asking the question which system truly promoted greater love toward God and neighbor? Christ as an exalted human whose example we ought to follow, or Christ as the divine Son of God who wrought salvation on our behalf with his own blood?

*Morality and the worship of Christ*
In the second letter of *Calvinistic and Socinian Systems Examined*, Fuller began his argument with an examination of which view of Christ is more likely to convert the worst kinds of sinners. Socinians such as Priestley had an emaciat-

---

[29] Fuller, *The Calvinistic and Socinian Systems Examined*, 2:111.

[30] A.H. Kirkby, *Andrew Fuller: A Heritage Biography* (Letchworth, Hertfordshire: Independent Press, 1961), 12–13.

[31] Fuller, *Calvinistic and Socinian Systems Examined*, 2:108–109. Also see Maddison and Maddison, "Joseph Priestley and the Birmingham Riots," 98.

ed view of the power of sin, which Fuller described as a "diminutive notions" of its evil.[32] Socinians like Priestley bemoaned the lack of vital piety among their congregations, yet they had undermined the basis for moral discipline through rejecting the deity of Christ and his salvific work. Sin must not be too terrible if the solution is to imitate the life of another man who was successfully obedient to God. Fuller quoted Priestley from his *Defense of Unitarianism* as saying that Priestley, "does not appear to consider him as 'the way of a sinner's salvation' in any sense whatsoever."[33] How could the Socinians claim that the doctrine of the deity of Christ caused moral corruption in the church when undermining that doctrine neutered the bite of sin?

Having shown the theological consequences of Socinianism, Fuller turned to practical reports from churches around England. Which congregations were seeing wonderful changes in the lives of sinners? Socinians, who proclaimed Christ as an example of obedience that men ought to imitate if they can, or Trinitarians, who urged the wicked to repent of their sins and trust in the Son of God who had died for them? Fuller pointed out that "Socinian writers cannot so much as pretend that their doctrine has been used to convert profligate sinners to the love of God and holiness," while miraculously reformed reprobates filled evangelical churches.[34]

In Letter VII, Fuller confronted Priestley's accusation that those who acclaimed Christ as God denied true worship to God the Father, who ought to be its sole object. Fuller found Priestley's attempt to guard God's glory disingenuous, as the Socinian scheme gives God "only a subordinate place in the system," since they contend that God's ultimate end is the good of all his creatures.[35] Fuller certainly did believe that Christians ought to guard God's glory. However, he pointed out that the earliest persecutors of the believers had used the same excuse to reject Christ's message. Had not Christ warned his disciples that those who persecuted them would do so thinking that they were serving God?

Priestley had argued that the earliest Christians did not worship or pray to Christ, yet Fuller pointed out a great difficulty with his position near the end of Letter VII. The very first Christian martyr, Stephen, had prayed to Christ even as he was dying, and the accounts in Scripture (which Priestley professed to take as authoritative) are full of instances of Christ being prayed too and worshipped as God.[36] When Thomas had first seen the risen Christ, his response

---

[32] Fuller, *Calvinistic and Socinian Systems Examined*, 2:116.

[33] Fuller, *Calvinistic and Socinian Systems Examined*, 2:118.

[34] Fuller, *Calvinistic and Socinian Systems Examined*, 2:119.

[35] Fuller, *Calvinistic and Socinian Systems Examined*, 2:159.

[36] Fuller, *Calvinistic and Socinian Systems Examined*, 2:160. Michael A.G. Haykin, "A Socinian and Cal-

had been to worship him as God, and Christ received the worship without rebuke.[37] The earliest Christians certainly had not believed that the worship of Christ was an idolatrous detraction from the worship due to God the Father.[38]

The final section of Fuller's work to be examined is Letter XI, in which Fuller connected biblical love for Christ with the affirmation of Christ's deity. Fuller drew the connection from this subject to his topic of Christian morality by noting that "love to Christ is one of the cardinal virtues of the Christian scheme," the fountain out of which all Christian morality flows.[39] Would not the system with the more exalted view of Christ have naturally promoted a more exalted love for him? Only orthodoxy "supposes him [Christ] to be equal or one with God," while Priestley's Socinianism "reduces him to the rank of a mere fellow creature."[40] Fuller, relying on the Scriptures that both he and Priestley professed to revere and follow, cited numerous passages from both the Old and New Testaments that utilized language for Christ that could only be applied to God, in order "to show that the primitive gospel was full of Christ … and that this, its leading and principle characteristic, tended wonderfully to promote the love of Christ," the greatest of Christian virtues.[41] Tom Nettles defined Fuller's argument as "conformity to morality itself … cannot exist apart from love to Christ."[42]

*Conclusion*

Both Andrew Fuller and Joseph Priestley sought to promote moral discipline and vital piety through religious practice. Priestley believed that the worship of Christ as God discredited Christianity and therefore stifled its ability to be a positive moral influence on rational men and women who had left superstition behind. The triune God was a corruption of early Christian belief that needed to be discarded if the faith were to persevere. Fuller rejected Priestley's

---

vinist Compared: Joseph Priestley and Andrew Fuller on the Propriety of Prayer to Christ," *Nederlands archief voor kerkgeschiedenis/Dutch Review of Church History* 72, no. 2 (1993): 192.

[37] Andrew Fuller, *The Atonement of Christ and the Justification of the Sinner. Arranged from the Writings of the Rev. Andrew Fuller. By the Editor of His Complete Works* (New York: The American Tract Society, 1854), 46–47.

[38] Fuller, *Calvinistic and Socinian Systems Examined*, 2:161.

[39] Fuller, *Calvinistic and Socinian Systems Examined*, 2:188.

[40] Fuller, *Calvinistic and Socinian Systems Examined*, 2:189.

[41] Fuller, *Calvinistic and Socinian Systems Examined*, 2:189–193.

[42] Tom J. Nettles, "Christianity Pure and Simple: Andrew Fuller's Contest with Socinianism," in *"At the Pure Fountain of Thy Word": Andrew Fuller as an Apologist*, ed. Michael A.G. Haykin (Carlisle, Cumbria: Paternoster, 2004), 155.

campaign, arguing instead that Christian morality could not be separated from Trinitarian doctrine. In particular, the divinity of Christ and his atoning death as the sinner's substitute (which rested on his divine nature) was the greatest motivator of love for Christ, which was itself the ultimate source of all Christian virtue. Priestley and anyone else who argued that directing worship and prayer toward Christ impeded Christian morality were themselves undermining the foundation for that morality.

# In the midst of his afflictions: Andrew Fuller as suffering missionary-theologian of the Spirit

Nicholas J. Abraham

Nicholas J. Abraham is a PhD candidate at The Southern Baptist Theological Seminary, the Lead Pastor/Planter at Reformation Bible Church in Navarre, Ohio, and Professor of Church History and Biblical Spirituality at Emmaus Theological Seminary in Cleveland, Ohio. He can be reached at nabraham@emmausseminary.org.

---

Andrew Fuller was a significant theologian for the modern overseas mission movement. Nevertheless, his theological contribution to that great endeavor was forged in a time of personal suffering and loss. To understand how Fuller's unique experience affected his contribution to the mission, this article seeks to read Fuller in his historical and theological contexts. Specifically, the following sections examine Fuller's trials and sufferings in the year that the Baptist mission emerged, his theological writings and sermons that fueled the formation of the Baptist Missionary Society (BMS), and an association circular letter Fuller wrote in 1810. These three areas manifest that Andrew Fuller was a missionary theologian of the Spirit, as his grasp of the work of the Holy Spirit formed his personal piety and in turn shaped his evangelistic zeal.

*Fuller's suffering in 1792*
At the beginning of 1792, Fuller wrote in his diary: "This year was begun, or nearly so, with a day of solemn fasting and prayer, kept by us as a church. It was a most affecting time with me and many more. Surely we never had such

a spirit of prayer amongst us!"[1] Unknown to him on that January day, the year 1792 would prove to be a most tumultuous year for him. The challenges began in April, as Fuller recalled that "on the 2d of April we lost our dear and worthy deacon, Mr. Beeby Wallis. The next church meeting was kept as a day of solemn fasting and prayer, and a very tender occasion it was."[2] Beeby Wallis (1735–1792) had introduced Fuller to the Kettering congregation and was instrumental in calling him to be the pastor.[3] Wallis' great grandfather, William Wallis, had served as the first pastor of the Kettering congregation when it was formed in 1696.[4] Beeby Wallis had faithfully served as a deacon for twenty-four years.[5] Fuller preached Wallis' funeral from Revelation 14:13, in which, Fuller referred to Wallis as a friend and expressed the difficulty he felt in speaking about such a loss.[6]

By June 1792, the trials continued within Fuller's own household, as Fuller's wife fell ill while being pregnant. Sarah Fuller (1756–1792) became mentally depressed since the loss of her daughter Sarah (1780–1786)—known as Sally—

---

[1] Andrew Fuller, "Memoir of Mr. Fuller," in *The Complete Works of Andrew Fuller*, ed. Joseph Belcher (1845; repr., Harrisonburg, VA: Sprinkle, 1988), 1:58.

[2] Fuller, "Memoir of Mr. Fuller," in *Works*, 1:58.

[3] Peter J. Morden, *The Life and Thought of Andrew Fuller (1754–1815)* (Milton Keynes, Buckinghamshire: Paternoster, 2015), 100.

[4] Morden, *Life and Thought of Andrew Fuller*, 70–71; Andrew Fuller, "The Blessedness of the Dead who Die in the Lord," in *Works*, 1:158.

[5] Fuller, "Blessedness of the Dead who Die in the Lord," in *Works*, 1:158.

[6] Fuller, "Blessedness of the Dead who Die in the Lord," in *Works*, 1:152. The church as well as the Wallis family requested that the funeral sermon be published to be distributed, which was first published as *The Blessedness of the Dead who Die in the Lord* (London: Dilly, Matthews, Ash, and Gardiner; Kettering: Collis; Northampton: Birdsall, 1792).

Fuller, "Blessedness of the Dead who Die in the Lord," in *Works*, 1:152. Belcher notes that Fuller planted a sycamore tree near Wallis's tomb and an inscription was placed on the tomb, written by Fuller:

Kind sycamore, preserve beneath thy shade
The precious dust of him who cherished thee;
Nor thee alone; a plant to him more dear
He cherished, and with fostering hand upreared.
Active and generous in virtue's cause,
With solid wisdom, strict integrity,
And unaffected piety, he lived
Beloved amongst us, and beloved he died.
Beneath an Allon-bachuth Jacob wept;
Beneath thy shade we mourn a heavier loss.

See *Works* 1:58n.

some years before.[7] Sally, one of two Fuller children to survive infancy up to that point, died on May 30, 1786, at the age of six.[8] Sarah, Fuller's wife, continued to struggle with this loss up until 1792, and her crippling sadness was compounded with physical maladies. Regarding the situation, Fuller reflected: "it was a thought, likewise, which lately struck me, that we have no more religion than what we have in times of trial. On this subject I preached from Exod xvi. 4. It seems as if these things were preparative to a time of trial for me."[9] Nothing but God's keeping grace given through the scriptures prepared Fuller for the loss he faced and would continue to face. Near the end of that summer, he lost his wife. On August 25, 1792, Fuller wrote to his father-in-law to give him news of his wife's death. Fuller recounted her mental anguish, fits of hysteria, and her eventual passing after the birth of their daughter. He wrote:

> On Thursday, the 23d instant, she was delivered of a daughter; but was all the day very restless, full of pain and misery no return of reason, except that from an aversion to me, which she had so long entertained, she called me 'my dear,' and twice kissed me; said she 'must die,' and 'let me die, my dear,' said she, 'let me die!' Between nine and ten o'clock, as there seemed no immediate sign of a change, and being very weary, I went to rest; but about eleven was called up again, just time enough to witness the convulsive pangs of death, which in about ten minutes carried her off.[10]

Fuller continued: "it is the cup which my Father hath given me to drink, and shall I not drink it?"[11] For the time being, Fuller was left alone in the ministry.[12] Fuller named his newborn daughter Bathoni after Rachel's final child in the Old Testament (Gen 35:16–18). Sadly, Bathoni only lived three weeks.[13] By September 1792, Fuller's experience of sorrow and loss increased. He aptly penned a poem a few months later reflecting on his grief. The last stanza stated:

---

[7] Morden, *Life and Thought of Andrew Fuller*, 101.

[8] Morden, *Life and Thought of Andrew Fuller*, 98–99.

[9] Fuller, "Memoir of Mr. Fuller," in *Works*, 1:58.

[10] Fuller, "Memoir of Mr. Fuller," in *Works*, 1:60–61.

[11] Fuller, "Memoir of Mr. Fuller," in *Works*, 1:61.

[12] Matthew Haste, "Marriage and Family in the Life of Andrew Fuller," *The Southern Baptist Journal of Theology* 17.1 (2013): 30. See the poem Fuller wrote on the one-year anniversary after Sarah's death. The last line read, "To weep unheeded, and to serve alone."

[13] Morden, *The Life and Thought of Andrew Fuller (1754–1815)*, 103.

> God of my life, and guide of all my years,
> May I again to thee my soul commend,
> And in thee find a Friend to share my griefs,
> And give me counsel in each doubtful path,
> And lead me on through every maze of life,
> Till I arrive where sighs no more are heard![14]

It is difficult to imagine how Fuller coped with his bereavement and agony, while he participated in the formation of the BMS and overseas mission. Peter Morden has rightfully argued that Fuller's suffering, especially as he recorded it in his diary, was real suffering, which is evidenced by his detailed descriptions.[15] His mental and spiritual state was a culmination of all that had transpired that year, compounded with his previous experiences of loss and spiritual struggle.[16]

## Founding of the BMS

A year earlier, on April 27, 1791, Fuller preached to an association meeting at Clipstone, Northamptonshire on Haggai 1:2.[17] In it, Fuller stated that "we see many things that should be done, but there are difficulties in the way, and we wait for these difficulties being all removed."[18] Though expediency and wisdom may call for caution at times, Fuller argued that nothing would ever happen if caution were always the posture of God's people. He went on to argue: "had Luther, and his contemporaries, acted upon this principle, they had never gone about the glorious work of Reformation."[19] While Fuller displayed his point of not allowing caution to hinder the work of God, he did not propose that God's people should pretend as if difficulties were not real; instead, he called for a change of perspective: "instead of waiting for the removal of difficulties, we

---

[14] Fuller, "Memoir of Mr. Fuller," in *Works*, 1:62.

[15] Peter J. Morden, "'So valuable a life ...': A Biographical Sketch of Andrew Fuller (1754-1815)," *The Southern Baptist Journal of Theology* 17.1 (2013): 9.

[16] Morden, "So valuable a life," 8-9. Morden shows that Fuller's diary shows that he was wrestling with a kind of spiritual depression in the years leading up to his wife Sarah's death and in the years leading up to his daughter Sally's death. This wrestling can be attributed to his introspective tendencies precipitated by his high Calvinist background. Such self-examination has been displayed in the diary of John Newton (1725-1807) in addition to the writing of other Puritans.

[17] Andrew Fuller, *The Pernicious Influence of Delay in Religious Concerns* (Clipstone: J.W. Morris, 1791), 17-30. Also see Fuller, "Instances, Evil, and Tendency of Delay, in the Concerns of Religion," in *Works*, 1:145-151.

[18] Fuller, *Pernicious Influence of Delay in Religious Concerns*, 20-21.

[19] Fuller, *Pernicious Influence of Delay in Religious Concerns*, 21.

ought in many cases to consider them as purposely laid in our way, in order to try the sincerity of our religion."[20] Here Fuller touched on a recurring theme in his life and ministry, that trials were at the sovereign behest of God to bring about his desired ends. It was at this point that Fuller issued a call to missions:

> Let it be considered whether it is not owing to this principle that so few and so feeble efforts have been made for the propagation of the gospel in the world.—When the Lord Jesus commissioned his apostle[s], he commanded them to Go, and teach all nations, to preach the gospel to every creature; and that notwithstanding the difficulties and oppositions that would lie in their way. The apostles executed their commission with assiduity and fidelity; but since their days we seem to sit down half contented that the greater part of the world should still remain in ignorance and idolatry. Some noble efforts indeed have been made, but they are but small in number when compared with the magnitude of the object. And why is it so? Are the souls of men of less value than heretofore? No. Is Christianity less true, or less important than in former ages? This will not be pretended. Are there no opportunities for societies, or individuals in Christian nations, to convey the gospel to the heathens? This cannot be pleaded so long as opportunities are found to trade with them, yea, and what is a disgrace to the name of Christians, to buy them, and sell them, and treat them with worse than savage barbarity! We have opportunities in abundance; the improvement of navigation, and the maritime and commercial turn of this country, furnish us with these? And it deserves to be considered, whether this is not a circumstance that renders it a duty peculiarly binding upon us.
>
> The truth is, if I am not mistaken, we wait for we know not what; we seem to think the time is not come, the time for the Spirit to be poured down from on high. We pray for the conversion and salvation of the world, and yet neglect the ordinary means by which those ends have been used to be accomplished ... Ought we not then to try, at least, by some means, to convey more of the good tidings of salvation to the world around us, than have hitherto been conveyed?[21]

Fuller's 1791 sermon promoted several theological concepts that became the foundation of the BMS. First, he argued, somewhat implicitly, that the Great Commission was binding on all believers. Second, the value of every

---

[20] Fuller, *Pernicious Influence of Delay in Religious Concerns*, 21.

[21] Fuller, *Pernicious Influence of Delay in Religious Concerns*, 22–23.

human being was expressed as a foundation to preach the gospel to all.[22] Third, he confessed the need for Christians to band together for this work of gospel ministry. Fourth, he saw the providence of the Lord displayed in the advances of technology and travel, both of which would improve missionary endeavors. Fifth, he declared the necessity of the Holy Spirit's empowerment in the task of missions. Finally, he saw the time as ripe for action. Yet, as Morden has stated, some additional time was needed after Fuller's message at the minister's meeting for the association to think through various logistical details.[23]

The importance of Fuller's message for the founding of the BMS has been debated in light of the message preached the following year by William Carey (1761–1834).[24] However, the chronology of the two messages displays Fuller's call to have preceded that of his Leicester friend. Carey's message, preached in May 1792, was the fruit of an essay that he had written some years prior. The essay, published as a pamphlet near the time of Carey's message, was entitled *An Enquiry into the Obligations of Christians to use Means for the Conversion of the Heathens*.[25] Fuller had read an early draft of Carey's essay before he preached at the minister's meeting in 1791. Therefore, Morden rightly noted the likely influence that Fuller had on Carey with his 1791 sermon and that Carey had on Fuller with the early draft of his essay along with his persistent missionary fervor.[26]

During Fuller's trying year in 1792, Carey preached his message at the Northamptonshire association meeting in May. Carey's message drove the association to action, wherein they passed a resolution to form what would become the BMS at their next meeting.[27] At the home of the recently bereaved widow of Beeby Wallis, Martha Wallis (1738–1812), on October 2, 1792, that meeting was held and the BMS was born.[28] It is astounding to ponder the men-

---

[22] Fuller plainly confessed this point in the statement of faith he drafted upon his call to Kettering. See Michael A.G. Haykin, ed., *The Armies of the Lamb: The spirituality of Andrew Fuller* (Dundas, ON: Joshua Press, 2001), 279.

[23] Morden, *Life and Thought of Andrew Fuller*, 118.

[24] Morden, *Life and Thought of Andrew Fuller*, 117–118.

[25] Morden, *Life and Thought of Andrew Fuller*, 118; Francis Augustus Cox, *History of the Baptist Missionary Society from 1792 to 1842* (London: T. Ward and G. & J. Dyer, 1842), 1:12.

[26] Morden, *Life and Thought of Andrew Fuller*, 119. Carey's fervor for mission can be traced back to an association meeting in 1786 wherein the young pastor asked those gathered whether the Great Commission compelled them to spread the gospel to all nations. Unfortunately, Carey's question did not receive a positive response. See Paul Brewster, *Andrew Fuller: Model Pastor-Theologian* (Nashville, TN: B&H Academic, 2010), 130.

[27] Cox, *History of the Baptist Missionary Society*, 1:17.

[28] Morden, *Life and Thought of Andrew Fuller*, 120.

tal and spiritual state Fuller had been in around the time of this meeting. Only months before, he had lost his wife and infant daughter. It thus appears that the events of Fuller's life in 1792 were providential in shaping him and forming his contribution to the founding of the BMS. Furthermore, Fuller's experience seemed to shape his broader work, even as it was revelatory of his theology. In his 1791 message, Fuller referred to the difficulties placed in the path of a believer as having been put there to test one's faith. In Andrew Gunton Fuller's (1799–1884) memoir, the son alluded to his father's state during this October 1792 meeting:

> The employments of life have been ranked among its greatest blessings; and never does their value appear more striking than when they are directed to the relief of a mind overwhelmed with distress. In conjunction with a few individuals, who had united with him in strenuous efforts to induce compassion on behalf of the heathen world, Mr. Fuller was, in the midst of his afflictions, occupied in maturing plans which issued in the formation of the "Particular Baptist Society for propagating the gospel among the heathen."[29]

As Fuller was "overwhelmed with distress" and "in the midst of his afflictions," he was appointed the BMS' first secretary and plans were made for Carey and John Thomas (1757–1801) to depart for India the next year.[30] Fuller's theological convictions along with his friendship with Carey propelled him to involvement.[31] The house in which this meeting took place is a precious detail—it was the house of Fuller's friend Beeby Wallis, who had died earlier that year. Fuller was grieving, but he was not the only grieving person there. While some have called the BMS a child of the Baptist association of which Fuller was a part, in some sense, grief served as a midwife to its founding.[32]

*Relying on the Spirit*
In the years leading up to the meeting that founded the BMS, Fuller had established himself as a prominent voice on the "Modern Question." Fundamentally, the "question" was whether the unconverted had a duty to believe in the gos-

---

[29] Fuller, "Memoir of Mr. Fuller," in *Works*, 1:62.

[30] Morden, *Life and Thought of Andrew Fuller*, 120.

[31] Michael A.G. Haykin, "Introduction," in Andrew Fuller, *The Works of Andrew Fuller*, ed. Andrew Gunton Fuller (Edinburgh: The Banner of Truth Trust, 2007), [2–3]. This "Introduction" in not paginated.

[32] Brian Stanley, *The History of the Baptist Missionary Society: 1792–1992* (Edinburgh: T&T Clark, 1992), 14.

pel.³³ In 1785, Fuller went into print answering in the affirmative in his work, *The Gospel Worthy of All Acceptance*.³⁴ However, Fuller was careful to state that sinners needed the Holy Spirit to enable them to perform this duty of belief.³⁵ Though sinners had this duty before them, they were not left to their own strength or power to obey this duty but were instead constrained to plead for the Holy Spirit's help. For some, answering the question in this way was perplexing. As Mark Noll points out, "to Baptist traditionalists, this proposition seemed to negate the force of God's sovereign call of election, since how could it be the duty of an ordinary sinner to repent if God was the sole agent in bringing unbelievers from spiritual death to spiritual life?"³⁶ Fuller argued, "in fine, the Scriptures uniformly teach us that all our sufficiency to do good or to abstain from evil is from above; repentance and faith, therefore, may be duties, notwithstanding their being the gifts of God."³⁷ Furthermore, he established this claim on the biblical premise that sin produced the inability to perform the duties prescribed by God. Such a claim ruled out the prospect of natural limitations keeping sinners from believing, which was an insight Fuller gained from reading Jonathan Edwards (1703–1758).³⁸ Thus, sinners must believe in the gospel, sinners can believe in the gospel by the power of the Holy Spirit, and this meant that the gospel must be preached to sinners. A natural product of such theological logic is mission.³⁹

As the effort of mission progressed, both in local churches and abroad, pastors and missionaries would need to rely on the empowerment of the Holy Spirit for any kind of lasting fruit. Part of the Spirit's work is to convict the world of sin and part of that conviction includes dealing with sinners who have not believed in the Son (see John 3:36, 16:9). Thomas Nettles has shown how Fuller integrated this need to believe in the Son and the Spirit's efficacious work

---

³³ Morden, *Life and Thought of Andrew Fuller*, 52; Geoffrey F. Nuttall, "Northamptonshire and 'The Modern Question:' A Turning Point in Eighteenth-Century Dissent," *Journal of Theological Studies* 16, no. 1 (1965): 102.

³⁴ Brewster, *Andrew Fuller*, 32–33.

³⁵ Andrew Fuller, *Gospel Worthy of All Acceptation*, in *Works*, 2:379.

³⁶ Mark Noll, *The Rise of Evangelicalism: The Age of Edwards, Whitefield and the Wesleys* (Downers Grove, IL: InterVarsity, 2003), 208.

³⁷ Fuller, *Gospel Worthy of All Acceptation*, in *Works*, 2:380.

³⁸ Fuller, *Gospel Worthy of All Acceptation*, in *Works*, 2:380; John Piper, *Andrew Fuller: Holy Faith, Worthy Gospel, World Mission* (Wheaton, IL: Crossway, 2016), 42; Morden, *Life and Thought of Andrew Fuller*, 62–63; Brewster, *Andrew Fuller*, 78.

³⁹ That is not to say that Fuller's perspective was the only impetus for mission, but that he was one of the key voices for it. See Morden, *Life and Thought of Andrew Fuller*, 109–110.

for belief.[40] Therefore, reliance on the Spirit to enable sinners to perform the duty of belief was necessary for pastors and parishioners as well as missionaries and the unreached. All were beholden to the Lord of life to give life (see John 6:63a; 2 Cor 3:6, 17).

*The promise of the Spirit*
Eighteen years after the BMS was established, Fuller was selected to write the circular letter for the Northamptonshire Association, entitled "The Promise of the Spirit the Grand Encouragement in Promoting the Gospel."[41] The main subject of the letter was to follow up the previous year's teaching on the Holy Spirit and discuss the Spirit's relationship to the work of evangelism. He argued that spreading the gospel should mark the lives of genuine believers, as "the true churches of Jesus Christ travail in birth for the salvation of men."[42] Fuller looked back over the time the BMS had been in operation and reflected on God's work of salvation accomplished abroad and at home. For Fuller, he could not leave out the powerful work of the Spirit in "the salvation of men."

Problems had arisen amongst the churches as to how the Holy Spirit was perceived. Some had relegated the Spirit to only extraordinary gifts. Others had assumed that the Spirit would do all the work in salvation, thus promoting laziness in evangelism.[43] In speaking to these problems, Fuller appealed to the main points set forth the previous year by Robert Hall, Jr. (1764–1831), who proclaimed the great need Christians have of the Holy Spirit and their needing to seek his help in prayer.[44] Fuller went on to show how the Old Testament gives numerous examples of the people of God relying on God.[45] Furthermore, he showed how "the success of the gospel in the times of the apostles is ascribed to the influence of the Holy Spirit, as its first or primary cause."[46] Fuller harkened back to an insight he had established in *Gospel Worthy of All Acceptation* that "if the success of the gospel were owing to the pliability of the people, or to

---

[40] Thomas J. Nettles, "The Passion and Doctrine of Andrew Fuller in 'The Gospel Worthy of All Acceptation,'" *The Southern Baptist Journal of Theology* 17, no. 2 (2013): 29.

[41] Andrew Fuller, "The Promise of the Spirit the Grand Encouragement in Promoting the Gospel," in *Works*, 3:359.

[42] Fuller, "Promise of the Spirit," in *Works*, 3:359.

[43] Fuller, "Promise of the Spirit," in *Works*, 3:359–360.

[44] Fuller, "Promise of the Spirit," in *Works*, 3:360.

[45] Fuller, "Promise of the Spirit," in *Works*, 3:360–361. He referenced Ps 90:16–17, 126:3; Jer 2:2–3; Hab 3:2; Zech 4:2, 6.

[46] Fuller, "Promise of the Spirit," in *Works*, 3:361. He referenced Acts 6:7, 11:21, 14:1, 16:14, 18:10; John 14:12; Matt 16:17, 28:20; 2 Cor 2:14, 10:4; James 5:13–16.

any preparedness, natural or acquired, for receiving it, we might have expected it to prevail most in those places which were the most distinguished by their morality, and most cultivated in their minds and manners."[47] The framework guided Fuller's argument is twofold: the distinction of moral and natural wills, and the necessity of the work of the Holy Spirit in conversion. Eighteen years since the formation of BMS, Fuller was as convinced as ever, both by scripture and by experience, that the "non-application, non-invitation scheme" of high Calvinism was wrong.[48] In other words, Fuller believed that the Holy Spirit's salvific work operates through the dutiful and necessary means of Christians' preaching of the gospel.

In the conclusion, Fuller pointed out that "this is the natural consequence of the doctrine. If all our help be in God, to him it becomes us to look for success."[49] Fuller called his fellow Baptists to follow the pattern of saints in the Old and New Testaments to call on God in prayer. In referring to the early disciples praying in the upper room and God responding with sending the Spirit at Pentecost, Fuller was likely thinking of what had occurred in their own day.[50] In 1784, the Northamptonshire Association heard a call to monthly prayer by John Sutcliff (1752–1814).[51] Fuller preached the sermon at that year's meeting and the call to prayer was later printed along with Fuller's sermon.[52] The call to prayer was specifically for meetings to be held on the first Monday of every month for specific times of prayer for revival. They were inspired by Jonathan Edwards' *Humble Attempt* (1747).[53] Fuller's mention of Edwards in his 1810 circular letter of prayer preceding Pentecost, may have been a veiled reference to the prayer meetings that preceded the founding and the work of the BMS.[54]

[47] Fuller, "Promise of the Spirit," in *Works*, 3:361.

[48] Brewster, *Andrew Fuller*, 73.

[49] Fuller, "Promise of the Spirit," in *Works*, 3:362.

[50] Fuller, "Promise of the Spirit," in *Works*, 3:362.

[51] Morden, *Life and Thought of Andrew Fuller*, 114.

[52] Andrew Fuller, *The Nature and Importance of Walking by Faith: A Sermon to which are added, A Few Persuasives to a General Union in Prayer for the Revival of Real Religion*, 2nd ed. (London: Vernor, 1791).

[53] Fuller, *Nature and Importance of Walking by Faith*, 37–38n. Jonathan Edwards, *An Humble Attempt to Promote Explicit Agreement and Visible Union of God's People in Extraordinary Prayer for the Revival of Religion and the Advancement of Christ's Kingdom on Earth, Pursuant to Scripture-Promises and Prophecies Concerning the Last Time* (Boston, 1747). Also see David W. Kling, "Edwards in the Context of International Revivals and Missions," in *The Oxford Handbook of Jonathan Edwards*, eds. Douglas A. Sweeney, and Jan Stievermann (Oxford: Oxford University Press, 2021), 58–60.

[54] The prayer meetings became a Particular Baptist mainstay in the years that followed the prayer call of 1784, but they also spread beyond Particular Baptist churches. See Morden, *Life and Thought of Andrew Fuller*, 114–115.

For Fuller, the church was to continue to ask of the Spirit for help in the Christian life and in mission.

The letter was closed out with Fuller's eschatological perspectives coming to the fore. In his postmillennial scheme, he saw the time as ripe: "The sum is, that the time for the promulgation of the gospel is come; and, if attended to in a full dependence on the promise of the Spirit, it will, no doubt, be successful."[55] Such a conclusion is derivative of a statement he made in *Gospel Worthy of All Acceptation* as he claimed that the problem of sin can only be overcome by God. Right before Fuller quoted John Calvin (1509–1564) to establish his point, he stated: "it is depravity only that renders the regenerating influence of the Holy Spirit necessary."[56] The remedy for a lost and unbelieving world, Fuller emphasized, is the gospel brought to light by the Spirit.[57]

*The union of suffering and mission: concluding thoughts*
In the fall of 1791, Fuller was reflecting on his own spiritual life and that of his fellow Christians:

> Oh to be spiritually alive among ourselves! One Monday evening, I think in October, I told our friends of some such things, and prayed with them with more than usual affection. I was particularly encouraged by the promise of giving the Holy Spirit to them that ask. Surely if ever I wrestled with God in my life I did so then, for more grace, for forgiveness, for the restoration of the joys of salvation; and that not only for myself, but for the generality of Christians among us, whom I plainly perceived to be in a poor lukewarm state, when compared with the primitive Christians.[58]

At one of the scheduled Monday evening prayer meetings, which had been happening for seven years before that October night, Fuller prayed for the Spirit's help. As the calendar turned to 1792, Fuller would need this friend, the Paraclete, to supply what he lacked. Yet, it seems that he was needing it even then. Here, Fuller's spirituality is shown to be directly linked to his views on mission. The prayer call of 1784 had not only been to appeal to God to act powerfully in mission, but to bring revival.[59] What it looked like for God to bring

---

[55] Fuller, "Promise of the Spirit," in *Works*, 3:363.

[56] Fuller, *Gospel Worthy of All Acceptation*, in *Works*, 2:380.

[57] Fuller, "Promise of the Spirit," in *Works*, 3:363.

[58] Fuller, "Memoir of Mr. Fuller," in *Works*, 1:57–58.

[59] Fuller, *Nature and Importance of Walking by Faith*, 37–38.

revival, in his grace and providence, was for him to build a mission engine that would run strong for years. The call to prayer that was published and distributed said as much:

> Add to all this, the prosperity of our souls as Christians, is generally connected with an earnest pursuit of God's glory and Christ's kingdom. Consolation, like reputation, won't do to be sought directly and for its own sake. In that case it will flee from us. But let us seek first the kingdom of God and his righteousness, and all these things will be added to us. One great reason perhaps of so many Christians going so destitute of divine comfort is because they care about scarcely anything else; God therefore justly with-holds it from them. If they were more to seek his glory, and the extending of his kingdom in the world, they would find consolation come of its own accord. He that cannot lie, speaking of his church, hath said, They shall prosper that love her.[60]

Seeking God and his kingdom was the priority for Fuller. He rightly saw this as how God worked in the hearts and lives of his people. The man who had suffered so deeply needed to call on God and trust in God's promise to give of his Spirit. The faithful secretary of the BMS reflected on God, the Holy Spirit's empowering presence in commissioning, sending, and establishing the work of their hands. Fuller rightly saw the link between his spirituality and his theology, as well as the link between his spirituality and his missiology. He trusted the sovereign God, the Holy Spirit with the care of his soul and thereby entrusted the souls of the unreached to the same Lord. Andrew Fuller was a missionary theologian, as first and foremost, he was a theologian of the Spirit. Through the scriptures and personal experiences, Fuller understood that the Spirit of God is the comforter as well as the Lord and giver of life (John 14:26; 2 Cor 3:6, 17), which was invaluable for his life and ministry. Thus, as he properly understood the Spirit's work in life, suffering, and salvation, he could not help but be driven to mission.

---

[60] Fuller, *Nature and Importance of Walking by Faith*, 47.

# Biblical meditation in the life of Andrew Fuller

Ronald C. Barnes

*Ronald C. Barnes earned his DMin at The Southern Baptist Theological Seminary, Louisville, KY. He is currently the lead pastor of Grand River Community Church in Elora, Ontario.*

*Introduction*
Andrew Fuller (1754–1815) was a Calvinistic pastor-theologian who had a monumental influence on evangelical Christianity in the eighteenth- and early nineteenth-centuries. His theological works were the catalyst that encouraged Calvinistic Baptist preachers to shift from their high Calvinism, to offering the gospel to lost sinners, inviting them to repent and trust in Christ alone for salvation. Fuller through works like *The Gospel Worthy of All Acceptation*, provided the biblical justification that encouraged not just evangelistic preaching, but personal evangelism and overseas missions.[1] This article examines the role that biblical meditation played in Andrew Fuller's life. It begins with an overview of his life. It considers his rich view of Scripture and finally his practice of biblical meditation. First consideration will be given to Fuller's personal piety and his practice of meditation as evidenced in his diary. This will be followed by an examination of several of his sermons.

*Fuller's view of Scripture*
Fuller, like the Puritans and seventeenth-century Calvinistic Baptists, held to

[1] Peter Morden, *Offering Christ to the World: Andrew Fuller (1754–1815) and the Revival of Eighteenth-Century Particular Baptist Life* (Carlisle, Cumbria: Paternoster, 2003), 139.

a high view of scripture. Soham was relatively isolated and Fuller was in some sense thrust into the role of pastor there, and so he learned to rely predominately on the scriptures. He regarded the scriptures as "the infallible standard of faith and practice."[2] Fuller commented on Hebrew 5:12 and the nature of the scriptures when he expounded on the phrase "the oracles of God." He wrote:

> It is a proper term by which the sacred Scriptures were denominated, strongly expressive of their Divine inspiration and infallibility; in them God speaks; and to them it becomes us to hearken.[3]

Fuller was deeply engaged with the historical tradition that flowed from Augustine (354–430) to John Calvin (1509–1564) through the Puritans and down to Jonathan Edwards (1703–1758). However, he gave full preference to the scriptures, and immersed himself in the Bible which was always predominant in his mind and heart.[4] Fuller described the chief importance of the scripture in this way, "Lord, thou hast given me a determination to take up no principle at second hand; but to search for everything at the pure fountain of thy word."[5] Concerning the extent of inspiration, Fuller stated: "It is certain that those who wrote the books which compose the Old and New Testaments profess to have been Divinely inspired."[6]

Fuller was convinced that the Holy Spirit was the ultimate author of the scriptures. He wrote that "the Old and New Testaments are dictated by one and the same Spirit."[7] Yet, Fuller recognized that this was not a direct dictation, but that the Holy Spirit worked through the human author to achieve the divine intent. Fuller found room for both the divine and human authors when considering the origin of scripture. He stated:

> It is true that, having been communicated through human mediums, we may expect them, in a measure, to be humanized; the peculiar turn and talents of each writer will be visible, and this will give them the character

---

[2] Andrew Fuller, *The Calvinistic and Socinian Systems Examined and Compared, as to Their Moral Tendency*, in *The Complete Works of Rev. Andrew Fuller, With A Memoir of his life by the Rev. Andrew Gunton Fuller* (1845; Harrisonburg, VA: Sprinkle, 1988), 2:196.

[3] Fuller, "The Nature and Importance of an Intimate Knowledge of Divine Truth," in *Works*, 1:160.

[4] John Piper, *Andrew Fuller: Holy Faith, Worthy Gospel, World Missions* (Wheaton, IL: Crossway, 2016), 29.

[5] Andrew Gunton Fuller, "Memoir," in *Works*, 1:20.

[6] Andrew Fuller, *Letter of Systematic Divinity*, in *Works*, 1:699.

[7] Fuller, *Letter of Systematic Divinity*, in *Works*, 1:700.

of variety; but, amidst all this variety, a mind capable of discerning the Divine excellence will plainly perceive in them the finger of God.[8]

It was because of his understanding of human limitations and fallibility, that Fuller insisted the work of the Holy Spirit was indispensable in the formation of God's Word. Concerning the human side of the authorship of scripture he wrote:

> As men, they were subject to human imperfections; if, therefore, they had not been influenced by Divine inspiration, blemishes of this kind must have appeared in their writings, as well as in those of other men.[9]

Before accepting the call to the Baptist congregation at Kettering, Fuller provided the church with articles of faith that demonstrated where he stood on various doctrines.[10] Another strong evidence to support Fuller's high view of scripture is clearly demonstrated in the second and third articles. He put it this way:

> II. Yet, considering the present state of mankind, I believe we needed a revelation of the mind of God, to inform us more fully of his and our own character, of his designs towards us, and will concerning us; and such a revelation I believe the Scriptures of the Old and New Testament to be, without excepting any one of its books; and a perfect rule for faith and practice.
>
> III. From this divine volume, I learn many things concerning God, which I could not have learned from the works of nature, and the same things in a more convincing light. Here I learn, especially, the infinitely amiable moral character of God. His holiness, justice, faithfulness, and goodness, are exhibited here in such a light, by his holy law and glorious gospel, as is nowhere else to be seen.[11]

Fuller was careful in his reading of theological works not to admit others "ideas uncritically but he consistently evaluated them against the standard of

---

[8] Andrew Fuller, *The Gospel Its Own Witness*, in *Works*, 2:68.

[9] Fuller, *Gospel Its Own Witness*, in *Works*, 2:71.

[10] Andrew J. Spencer, "Andrew Fuller and the Doctrine of Revelation," *Southwestern Journal of Theology* 57, no. 2 (2015): 213; Paul Brewster, *Andrew Fuller: Model Pastor-Theologian* (Nashville: B&H Academic, 2010), 49.

[11] Brewster, *Andrew Fuller*, 50.

the Bible."[12] This is evidenced in a response that he sent to acknowledge a gift of books that he received from John Ryland, Jr. (1753–1825).[13] Ryland had sent some American theological works and Fuller bristled at one of those in a letter he forwarded to Ryland. He said:

> I received your parcel, containing several American publications. I have not had time to read them through, though I have looked over some of them. I did not quite like Mr. Bell's mode of appealing to the "unerring oracles of true philosophy and the word of God." God's Word is or is not, a sufficient rule, from whence the man of God may be thoroughly furnished. What is philosophy that it should become an "oracle," by which to try sentiments in divinity?[14]

Regarding theology, Fuller was convinced that an internally consistent system was important. Yet, he was always cognizant that such consistency could not be purchased at the expense of giving due consideration to the Bible. Throughout his ministry, Fuller remained a thoroughgoing biblicist.[15] He gave guidance concerning the reading of scripture in this manner: "[Read] the Bible not with a system before your eyes, but as a little child with humility and prayer."[16] He warned the Baptist Association of perils of theological imitation.[17] In considering some of reasons for downturn in the denomination, he wrote:

> Another cause of declension, we apprehend, is *making the religion of others our standard, instead of the Word of God.*—The Word of God is the only safe rule we have to go by, either in judging what is real religion, or what exertions and services for God are incumbent upon us.[18]

Fuller found the ultimate solution to any controversy in the pages of scripture. He noted:

---

[12] Nigel David Wheeler, "Eminent Spirituality and Eminent Usefulness: Andrew Fuller's (1754–1815) Pastoral Theology in his Ordination Sermons" (PhD diss., University of Pretoria, 2009), 20.

[13] Brewster, *Andrew Fuller*, 47–48.

[14] Michael A.G. Haykin, ed., *The Armies of the Lamb: The spirituality of Andrew Fuller* (Dundas, ON: Joshua Press, 2001), 139.

[15] Brewster, *Andrew Fuller*, 45.

[16] Haykin, ed., *Armies of the Lamb*, 217.

[17] Brewster, *Andrew Fuller*, 46.

[18] Andrew Fuller, *Expository Discourses on the Book of Genesis*, in *Works*, 3:21.

The sacred Scriptures contain the decisions of the Judge of all, both as things and characters, from which there is no appeal: nor is it fit there should be; seeing they are not only formed in wisdom, but perfectly accord with truth and equity.[19]

The study of scripture was not for the purpose of just gathering theological knowledge and satisfy our curious interests. The scriptures are meant to change us. Fuller wrote:

There is nothing in the sacred Scriptures to gratify idle curiosity; but much that commends itself to the conscience, and that interests the heart. They are a mirror into which he that seriously looks must, in a greater or less degree, see his own likeness, and discover what kind of character he is.[20]

The examination of scripture was to be done carefully. Fuller understood that there were hermeneutical rules that needed to be followed to properly interpret scripture. He recognized the importance of interpreting in a manner that carefully reflected the authorial intent of the text and not the mere words of the text.[21] As he stated:

If the sacred writings be not received for the purposes for which they were professedly given, and for which they were actually appealed to by Christ and his apostles, they are in effect rejected; and those who pretend to embrace them for other purposes will themselves be found to have passed the boundaries of Christianity, and to be walking in the paths of infidelity.[22]

The sermons that Fuller preached and his instructions to young pastors on how to prepare sermons, also demonstrated the high view of scripture that Fuller adhered to. Fuller encouraged young pastors to preach a chapter-by-chapter exposition of the Bible. He argued that this was critical because,

In going over a book, I have frequently been struck with surprise in meeting with texts which, as they had always occurred to me, I had understood in a sense utterly foreign from what manifestly appeared to be

---

[19] Andrew Fuller, *Letters on Systematic Divinity*, in *Works*, 1:702.

[20] Fuller, *Letters on Systematic Divinity*, in *Works*, 1:701.

[21] Andrew Fuller, *Thoughts on Preaching*, in *Works*, 1:713.

[22] Andrew Fuller, *Calvinist and Socinian Systems*, in *Works*, 2:231.

their meaning when viewed *in connexion with their context*.²³

Fuller appreciated that the context of a passage had to be understood in order to have proper interpretation, and careful exposition of whole books of the Bible was a means to ensure that the interpreter was acknowledging and interpreting in light of the context. The centrality of the Word was expressed through Fuller's sermons. Each sermon would begin with a key text, as was typical of that time. The sermon was customarily constructed based on the structure of the text. His 1809 sermon from Psalm 40:6–8 is a good example of this. The sermon had the title "Jesus the True Messiah." There were four main points and each point was drawn from a key phrase in the text.²⁴ Since Fuller was committed to a high view of scripture, it was his common practice to systematically expound his way through a book of the Bible in Sunday morning services.²⁵ He stayed faithful to this task throughout his ministry, so that before his death, "he expounded a large portion of the books of the Old and New Testament."²⁶

*Biblical meditation in the personal life of Andrew Fuller*
Fuller believed that the spiritual discipline of biblical meditation was of prime importance. His high view of scripture motivated him personally to meditate on the Bible and to instruct others to do the same. He wrote:

> The sacred Scripture is a rich mine abounding with substantial treasures, but it is a mine that must be *worked*. If we would read it to advantage, it must be with *prayer* and *meditation* … A blessing is pronounced upon the man *who meditates in God's law by day and by night.*²⁷

Fuller recognized that what Christians read and think about will shape and mold them. For that reason, it was critical for believers to meditate on scripture and to have our closest associations with those who followed Christ. Christ is the image of God and therefore our greatest theme for meditation. Fuller quoted his good friend Samuel Pearce (1766–1799) who put it this way:

---

²³ Fuller, *Thoughts on Preaching*, in *Works*, 1:712.

²⁴ Fuller, *Sermons and Sketches*, in *Works*, 1:210–220.

²⁵ Brewster, *Andrew Fuller*, 46.

²⁶ Fuller, "Memoir," in *Works*, 1:112.

²⁷ Andrew Fuller, *The Works of Andrew Fuller, in Eight Volumes* (New Haven, CT: S. Converse, 1824), 8:17–18.

> As our minds are insensibly assimilated by the books we read, and the company we keep, so it will be in reading the book of God, and associating with his people; and as the glory of God is manifested in the highest degree in the face of Jesus Christ, this is our principle theme for our meditation.[28]

Fuller believed that biblical meditation was an indispensable spiritual discipline for one who was in ministry. He was convinced that it was necessary for every minister to ingest scripture for spiritual nourishment if they would be successful. This was because he saw a direct correlation between personal piety an effectiveness in ministry.[29] Fuller saw to two primary objectives of a preacher. They are to *enlighten* the mind and *affect* the hearts of his hearers.[30] The Holy Spirit used the preaching of the Word to accomplish these objectives. This understanding was in correlation with the Puritan and seventeenth-century Calvinistic Baptist understanding of human nature as being tripartite and consisting of the mind, affections, and the will. To have a lasting effect preaching, and biblical meditation must first enlighten the mind, but it must also descend to the heart if it was to transform the will of the believer. For a pastor to enlighten the mind and affect the heart it was necessary that the Word do this work through the power of the Holy Spirit in his own heart first. Fuller wrote:

> We must meditate on these things *as Christians,* first feeding our own souls upon them, and then imparting that which we have believed and felt to others; or, whatever good we may do to them, we shall receive none ourselves. Unless we mix faith with what we preach, as well as with what we hear, the word will not profit us.[31]

So the aim of preaching was not simply to impart orthodox truths to the mind. Rather the goal was to help those people *feel* biblical truths and to appropriate them deep into the heart so that they would live out the truths. Therefore, if a pastor did not *feel* these truths through the process of his own meditation and teaching, he could not excite emulation in his hearers, since these affections are communicated through the preacher's own intense love for Jesus.[32]

Biblical meditation was the means by which the believer's mind was renewed

---

[28] Fuller, *Works of Andrew Fuller,* 7:363.

[29] Andrew Fuller, *The Influence of the Presence of Christ on a Minister,* in *Works,* 1:505.

[30] Fuller, *Faith in the Gospel a Necessary Prerequisite to Preaching* in Complete *Works,* 1:517.

[31] Fuller, *Preaching Christ* in Complete *Works,* 1:501.

[32] Fuller, *Ministers Should be Concerned not to be Despised* in *Works,* 1:489.

and the means to be filled with the full presence of God. Fuller wrote: "There is no room for the fulness of God in the unrenewed mind: it is pre-occupied with other things."[33] To assist the Christian so that his mind was not pre-occupied but able to focus, Fuller, like the Puritans and seventeenth-century Calvinistic Baptists, encouraged solitude. Fuller commented on Genesis 24:61–63, when Isaac was walking outside as Abraham's servant and Rebekah were approaching. Fuller stated:

> They are unexpectantly met by a person taking an evening walk. This was no other than Isaac. It may be thought that he was looking out, in hope of meeting them; but we are expressly told that his walk was for another purpose, namely, to *meditate*. He was a man of reflection and prayer; and in the cool of the evening it might be common for him to retire an hour to converse, as we would say, with himself, and with his God.[34]

Again like the Puritans and seventeenth-century Particular Baptists, Fuller recommended the morning as the best time to practice biblical meditation. In his work, *Reading the Scriptures*, Fuller gave advice regarding when and how to engage with the Scriptures:

> In the first place, I have found it good to appoint *set times* for reading the Scriptures; and none have been so profitable as part of the season appropriated to private devotion on rising in the morning. The mind at this time is reinvigorated and unencumbered. To read a part of the Scriptures, previous to prayer, I have found to be very useful. It tends to collect the thoughts, to spiritualize the affections, and to furnish us with sentiments wherewith to plead at a throne of grace. And as reading assists prayer, so prayer assists reading. At these seasons we shall be less in danger of falling into idle speculations, and of perverting Scripture in support of hypotheses. A spiritual frame of mind, as Mr. [Samuel] Pearce somewhere observes, is as a good light in viewing a painting; it will not a little facilitate the understanding of the Scriptures. I do not mean to depreciate the labours of those who have commented on the sacred writings; but we may read expositors, and consult critics, while the "spirit and life" of the word utterly escape us. A tender, humble, holy frame is perhaps of more importance to our entering into the mind of the Holy Spirit than all other means united. It is thus that, by "an unction from the Holy One, we know all things."

---

[33] Fuller, *Works of Andrew Fuller*, 4:128.

[34] Fuller, *Works of Andrew Fuller*, 5:213.

In reading by myself, I have also felt the advantage of being able to pause, and think, as well as pray; and to inquire how far the subject is any way applicable to my case, and conduct in life.[35]

In addition to recommending the morning, Fuller suggested that reading and meditation on Scripture be interchanged with prayer to have the greatest spiritual benefit. Again, he followed the pattern of the Puritans and seventeenth-century Calvinistic Baptists in this practice. The other important aspect was to prepare oneself for meditation by preparing the mind by getting into a spiritual frame. This is also, like the Puritans and Calvinistic Baptists that preceded Fuller, who both spoke of the need to engage in offering repentance to God before engaging in biblical meditation.

Fuller documented many aspects of his personal piety, including his practice of biblical meditation in his personal diary. On Saturday November 13, 1784, he wrote: "Much employed in meditation, but little spirituality today."[36] On Saturday, December 4, 1784, he wrote: "No manner of spirituality, though some freedom in meditation."[37] On Saturday February 19, 1785, Fuller wrote in his diary, "Some tender and good feelings this morning, feel an earnest desire that my mind might be well furnished with gospel sentiments. Some meditations affording some pleasure on Revelation 1:18."[38] Fuller wrote the following in his diary entry of Monday December 19, 1785: "Some pleasant thoughts likewise on Hebrews 2—It *became* him for who are all things &c preparative for the Lord's Supper."[39] These entries in his diary reveal that biblical meditation was a daily spiritual discipline in Fuller's life.

In his practice of biblical meditation, Fuller spent considerable time. Biblical meditation was not something that was accomplished in a few minutes. In his diary entry of Saturday, March 5, 1785, Fuller wrote, "Much employed in calls on friends. Some few hours in meditation."[40] The inference from this entry is that if Fuller had not been occupied in the pastoral visits to friends he would have spent more than a few hours in meditation.

In several candid entries, Fuller shared that the task of biblical meditation did not always prove to be profitable. His frustration and disappointment he

---

[35] Andrew Fuller, *Reading the Scriptures*, in *Works*, 3:788.

[36] Michael D. McMullen, and Timothy D. Whelan, eds., *The Diary of Andrew Fuller, 1780–1801*, The Complete Works of Andrew Fuller, Volume 1 (Berlin: Walter de Gruyter, 2016), 89.

[37] McMullen and Whelan, eds., *The Diary of Andrew Fuller*, 94.

[38] McMullen and Whelan, eds., *The Diary of Andrew Fuller*, 110.

[39] McMullen and Whelan, eds., *The Diary of Andrew Fuller*, 163.

[40] McMullen and Whelan, eds., *The Diary of Andrew Fuller*, 112.

recorded in several entries. On Saturday, June 5, 1784, Fuller wrote: "But a poor day in meditation—what a poor, barren creature I am!"[41] On Saturday, February 5, 1785, he wrote: "But a poor day in meditation. Surely mine is a wretched, barren life."[42] On Saturday, June 25, 1785, he recorded: "An uncommon load lies all day upon my spirits. Alas I am forced to read my sin in my affliction of mind. I'm incapable of all profitable meditation."[43] Similarly, on Saturday, June 25, 1785, Fuller wrote his diary, "But a poor day today in meditation."[44] On Saturday, October 30, 1781, he wrote, "Some pleasure today, but not much in meditation, on the love of Christ."[45] Again on Saturday, November 6, 1784, Fuller recorded, "Some pleasure today in meditation, but not much. *O will thou not revive us again?*"[46]

In his diary entries Fuller shows a pattern of spending considerable time on Saturdays in biblical meditation in preparation for preaching on the Lord's day. On Saturday, November 27, 1784, Fuller wrote, "Some pleasure in some thoughts on the second Psalm, on *joy & trembling.*"[47] In his entry the following day he recorded, "Much tenderness and pleasure in preaching on the above subject before the Lord's supper."[48] He confirmed that this was his regular practice in his entry from Friday, October 15, 1784, where he recorded, "Chiefly employed today in meditation for preaching."[49] On Saturday, March 12, 1785 he recorded, "But a poor day thinking of Isaiah 35."[50] In the next day's entry he recorded, "Some pleasing in preaching today on God's working in us to *will and to do* but a poor afternoon from Isaiah 35."[51] These two entries openly reveal that when Fuller struggled to meditate on the text for a message on Sunday, that the resulting message was not of the quality that he would hope for.

In his diary entries Fuller demonstrated that he practiced biblical meditation regarding a variety of passages and topics. On Saturday, June 24, 1780,

---

[41] McMullen and Whelan, eds., *The Diary of Andrew Fuller*, 53.

[42] McMullen and Whelan, eds., *The Diary of Andrew Fuller*, 106.

[43] McMullen and Whelan, eds., *The Diary of Andrew Fuller*, 133.

[44] McMullen and Whelan, eds., *The Diary of Andrew Fuller*, 137.

[45] McMullen and Whelan, eds., *The Diary of Andrew Fuller*, 85.

[46] McMullen and Whelan, eds., *The Diary of Andrew Fuller*, 87.

[47] McMullen and Whelan, eds., *The Diary of Andrew Fuller*, 92.

[48] McMullen and Whelan, eds., *The Diary of Andrew Fuller*, 92.

[49] McMullen and Whelan, eds., *The Diary of Andrew Fuller*, 82.

[50] McMullen and Whelan, eds., *The Diary of Andrew Fuller*, 114.

[51] McMullen and Whelan, eds., *The Diary of Andrew Fuller*, 114.

Fuller wrote:

> I have been thinking today of Isaiah 2:11 I have reason to be humbled, for I have so little humility: yet I think I have tasted a sweetness in that plan of redemption which strains the pride of all flesh.[52]

The text he focused on reads, "The lofty looks of man shall be humbled, and the haughtiness of men shall be bowed down, and the LORD alone shall be exalted in that day" (Isa 2:11, KJV). Fuller in his meditation on the passage applied it to himself, as he considered that there were circumstances or causes in his life for which he needed to be humbled. This diary entry, along with several similar entries, revealed that Fuller did not simply meditate on text to prepare a message for others, but first applied it to himself. One of the topics that Fuller would spend time meditating on were characteristics of God's law. He recorded the following in his diary entry of Saturday, October 14, 1780, "Solemn thoughts, on holiness, justness, and goodness of the law of God."[53] Another topic of meditation found in his diary concerned the nature of the spiritual growth of a Christian. Fuller wrote this on Saturday, March 3, 1781, "A very affecting time, in thinking on the growth of a Christian—that those who grow most in grace, are far from thinking themselves to be eminent Christians."[54] Fuller would contemplate key scriptural phrases and he received spiritual benefit in doing so. On Monday, April 26, 1784, he wrote: "Some fresh thoughts from "Take, eat" [Mt. 26.26]—O how desirable not to be a mere *spectator* in religion!"[55]

Puritan and seventeenth-century Calvinistic Baptists had promoted biblical meditation as a way of redeeming time. Fuller also made profitable use of his time by practicing biblical meditation when he travelled to various locations. In his diary entry of Saturday, November 20, 1784, he wrote:

> Thought on the first Psalm in my return from Gretton for tomorrow; but how unlike am I to the character their drawn! *My leaf seems to wither* every day, and scarce anything I do seems to prosper. Feel reflections for my want of *close walk with God*. Surely I need to renew Covenant, as it were, with God.[56]

---

[52] McMullen and Whelan, eds., *The Diary of Andrew Fuller*, 4.

[53] McMullen and Whelan, eds., *The Diary of Andrew Fuller*, 17.

[54] McMullen and Whelan, eds., *The Diary of Andrew Fuller*, 25.

[55] McMullen and Whelan, eds., *The Diary of Andrew Fuller*, 42.

[56] McMullen and Whelan, eds., *The Diary of Andrew Fuller*, 90.

Fuller made it a practice of actively thinking about scripture passages and especially how they applied to him, while engaging in his travel. We see in this extract above that as he contemplated on Psalm 1, he thought of how it applied to him and how he wanted to see change come in his life so that he might prosper in a closer walk with God. He wrote of another occasion of travel in his diary entries from Monday, February 28 to Friday, March 4, 1785:

> Called at Mrs. Hobsons, with whom I have some savory conversation. Riding from there to N[orthhampto]n had some pleased exercise from 1 Peter 1:6, *if need be ye are in heaviness &*.[57]

Fuller demonstrates through some of his diary entries that he would take time to meditate and pray in response to encounters with other believers and the new opportunities for learning and growth that resulted. Fuller heard about a "revival of religion" that was taking place in the lives of some in Walgrave and Guilsborough, and learned that this was connected with the intentional setting apart days for fasting and prayer. In response to this he wrote in his diary in 1791:

> I was particularly affected with this though by finding it in the 67th Psalm which I was expounding about the same time—"that God being merciful to *us* & blessing *us* might be the means of his way being known upon earth, and his saving health among all nations"; at least amongst a part of them.[58]

When hearing of God working a measure of revival among other believers, Fuller turns to the Scripture and meditates upon it to seek some appropriate answers and application for his context. Fuller personally looked for answers and appropriate responses through careful reflection on Scripture. Fuller was prepared to learn more about meditation and prayer from his interaction with other Christians. In his diary entry of April 20, 1785, he noted:

> Last Monday I heard a young man at Northampton speak of the advantage of mixing prayer with reading the word. This morning I have been trying to read in that way. Read over the second chapter of Hosea in this way.[59]

---

[57] McMullen and Whelan, eds., *The Diary of Andrew Fuller*, 112.

[58] McMullen and Whelan, eds., *The Diary of Andrew Fuller*, 181.

[59] McMullen and Whelan, eds., *The Diary of Andrew Fuller*, 125.

Through this diary entry Fuller demonstrated that the discipline of biblical meditation combined with prayer was one that continued to grow and develop in his life.

One of the hindrances to effective biblical meditation that the Puritans and seventeenth-century Reformed Baptists documented was the problem of a mind that was carried away with worldly and idle thoughts. Fuller expressed in several places in his personal diaries his struggle to focus in order to meditate. In his entry of July 11, 1780, Fuller wrote: "The cares of the world have engrossed my attention this afternoon."[60] On Saturday, August 14, 1784, Fuller wrote, "When I should be thinking on the word for the Lord's day how ready is my mind for other things."[61] In a similar manner his entry on August 28, 1784, stated, "My wandering mind how it roves after things when I should be attending to the work of the Lord's Day."[62] Again on Saturday, September 4, 1784, Fuller wrote, "Feel a great propensity to wandering of mind—seem as if I could think of almost anything but what I should."[63] In a similar manner he wrote on September 25, 1784, "I find it hard work to bend my mind to close thought."[64] On February 16, 1790, Fuller wrote, "For these last three weeks I have too much relapsed again into a state of thoughtlessness."[65] In addition Fuller put this entry in his diary that covered Monday, August 29, to Wednesday August 31: "for these two days past especially my mind has been wretchedly carnal. That passage has brought some conviction to me of late, 'Are you not *carnal*, and walk as men!'"[66] This struggle to focus was overcome for Fuller, by exercising perseverance in efforts to practice biblical meditation. An example of this is recorded in Fuller's diary entry for July 15, 1780: "my powers are all shackled, my thoughts contracted. Bless the Lord! I have felt a melting sense of the heinous nature of backsliding from the Lord, while thinking on Jeremiah 2:5, 31–33."[67]

Fuller described in many parts of his diary how biblical meditation was more than just the gathering of knowledge to contemplate with the mind. The scriptures that Fuller pondered touched him deeply and worked powerfully on his affections. His experience of having his affections warmed follows closely

---

[60] McMullen and Whelan, eds., *The Diary of Andrew Fuller*, 8.

[61] McMullen and Whelan, eds., *The Diary of Andrew Fuller*, 67.

[62] McMullen and Whelan, eds., *The Diary of Andrew Fuller*, 71.

[63] McMullen and Whelan, eds., *The Diary of Andrew Fuller*, 73.

[64] McMullen and Whelan, eds., *The Diary of Andrew Fuller*, 77.

[65] McMullen and Whelan, eds., *The Diary of Andrew Fuller*, 179.

[66] McMullen and Whelan, eds., *The Diary of Andrew Fuller*, 150.

[67] McMullen and Whelan, eds., *The Diary of Andrew Fuller*, 8.

the experiences of the Puritans and seventeenth-century Calvinistic Baptists. In his diary entry of Friday, June 16, 1780, he wrote: "Felt the importance of religion, and the desire of seeing the glory of Christ, and being conformed to his image. Saw a beauty in Ecclesiastes 12:13, 'Fear God, and keep the commandments for this is the whole of man.'"[68] On Thursday, June 22, 1780, Fuller in a similar manner wrote, "O that I might feel more of the power of religion, and know more of the love of Christ which passeth knowledge!"[69] He wrote about an encounter he experienced with God through meditation focused on Colossian 1:19: "O blessed be God, he has appeared once again. Tonight, while I prayed to him, how sweet was Colossians 1:19 to me. That which has pleased the Father pleases me. I am glad that all fullness dwells in Him."[70]

During those occasions when his mood was low, Fuller could receive benefit not just in his thinking, but a change in his affections and mood through biblical meditation. One example of this is from his diary entry of March 30, 1781: "Much melancholy gloom today; yet some melting thoughts on the astonishing provision of divine love. Several passages seemed sweet to me—'God is welling the hears of the proves should have strong consolation. If any one sin, we have an Advocate with the Father.'"[71] As Fuller meditated on passages, he asked a variety of questions and examined a text the way someone might examine a jewel by turning it over and over in the light to see every beautiful angle. As he did this, the scripture would ignite his affections as well as his intellect. An example of this can be found in his diary entry of Thursday, August 16, 1781. He wrote: "Serious, and somewhat pleasant. Wrote some thoughts on the holy angels taking pleasure in looking into our redemption. The end of predestination seemed sweet to me; namely, conformity to the image of God's dear Son."[72] On the Lord's day, August 12, 1781, Fuller wrote this entry in his diary, "Had a sweet forenoon, in thinking on the meditation of Christ and preaching upon that subject, from Ephesians 2:13."[73] This entry again demonstrates that Fuller would meditate in preparation for preaching and that he had the goal of being affected himself by the text before delivering it in a sermon. The strength of the impact on Fuller's affections was at times particularly strong. On August 11, 1781, Fuller wrote: "Have been ravished, as it were, today, in reading the account of the council held by the apostles and elders, Acts 15. Oh the beauty and

---

[68] McMullen and Whelan, eds., *The Diary of Andrew Fuller*, 2.

[69] McMullen and Whelan, eds., *The Diary of Andrew Fuller*, 3.

[70] McMullen and Whelan, eds., *The Diary of Andrew Fuller*, 15.

[71] McMullen and Whelan, eds., *The Diary of Andrew Fuller*, 26.

[72] McMullen and Whelan, eds., *The Diary of Andrew Fuller*, 33.

[73] McMullen and Whelan, eds., *The Diary of Andrew Fuller*, 33.

simplicity of primitive Christianity!"[74] A similar entry was recorded on Saturday, September 22, 1781: "My heart much moved this morning. Psalm 123:1, 2 was somewhat to me. Overcome in prayer, that God would shine upon my path. O God, thou knowest that I am willing to be any thing. It is my unfeigned desire, that not my will, but thine be done."[75]

On August 27, 1784, Fuller recorded this entry in his diary, "Some sweetness now for some days in reading over the *Acts of the Apostles*, before family prayer. Sweet times in that duty. O that we might see some such blessed times come over again!"[76] In the entry for Tuesday, July 20, 1784, he demonstrated again how he combined biblical meditation with prayer, and how this enhanced the impact the meditation had on his affections. He wrote, "Read the 9th chapter of John this morning with pleasure—went to prayer after it with solemn pleasure."[77] One primary topic that Fuller focused on in meditation was divine love and the blood of Christ, Fuller wrote the following in his diary entry on the Lord's day, July 2, 1780:

Surely, my views of myself, of divine love, and of the blood of Christ, never were clearer, nor yielded me greater satisfaction, than last night and today. Well, it has been a time of refreshment of the soul. Oh that I could retain the ideas I have had today! I thought God was such an intimately lovely being, that it was a great sin not to love him with our whole hearts. I thought one perpetual flame of supreme love was his natural due from every intelligent creature, and the want of such love merits damnation.[78]

Fuller engaged in soliloquy as part of the process of biblical meditation. This is similar to the practice of the Puritans and seventeenth-century Particular Baptists. Fuller would try and engage his own heart and soul by asking himself questions. An example of this is recorded in his diary entry of Thursday, July 12, 1781. At this time, he was considering leaving the Soham church and wanted to be sure he had pure and proper motives. He recorded the following: "have been trying today, to examine my heart by putting myself to such questions as these:—'Would it be most agreeable to my conscience to continue, after all, with my people?—Is it likely, in so doing, I should please God, and contribute

---

[74] McMullen and Whelan, eds., *The Diary of Andrew Fuller*, 33.

[75] McMullen and Whelan, eds., *The Diary of Andrew Fuller*, 35.

[76] McMullen and Whelan, eds., *The Diary of Andrew Fuller*, 70.

[77] McMullen and Whelan, eds., *The Diary of Andrew Fuller*, 64.

[78] McMullen and Whelan, eds., *The Diary of Andrew Fuller*, 6.

to the welfare of his cause, on the whole?"[79]

There were times when Fuller moved away from soliloquy to engage in discussion with other believers, especially the "spiritual friends" he had developed. The goal was to grow together through biblical meditation and dialogue concerning how to apply the truths they were learning. Fuller recorded an example of this in his diary entry of September 30, 1785:

> The best part of the day was I think in conversation. A question was put and discussed, to the following support ... "*To what causes in ministers may much of the want of their success be imputed?*" The answer much turned upon the want of *personal* religion—particularly the want of close dealing with God in *closet prayer.* Another reason assigned was, the want of reading and studying the Scriptures more as *Christians*, for the edification of our own souls. We are apt to study them merely to find out something to *say to others,* without living upon the truth ourselves. If we eat not the book before we deliver its contents to others, we may expect the Holy Spirit will not much accompany us. If we study the Scriptures as *Christians*, the more familiar we are with them, the more we shall feel their importance; but if otherwise our familiarity with the word will be like that of soldiers and doctors with death, it will wear away all sense of its importance from our minds.[80]

This entry demonstrates that Fuller was greatly blessed by engaging in spiritual conversations to ignite personal piety among brothers in Christ. The entry also indicates how important both Fuller and his friends felt their personal practice of biblical meditation was. It was imperative that their own hearts are impacted with spiritual truth before it should be passed on through their preaching and teaching.

Biblical meditation was a source of great spiritual benefit to Fuller. It was the meditation on scripture that caused an increase in Fuller's personal happiness and joy. On Thursday, March 29, 1781, he wrote: "thoughts on the advocateship of Christ, from John 16:7, and 14:2, have been precious to me: and of his prophetic office, from Matthew 17:5, "This is my beloved Son—*hear him.* What a wonder I am to myself! Compared with what I deserve to be, how happy my condition; compared with what I desire to be, how miserable!"[81] Biblical meditation is what gave Fuller strength and support through the greatest trials of his life. When Fuller's first wife Sarah was ill and suffering with a mental illness

---

[79] McMullen and Whelan, eds., *The Diary of Andrew Fuller*, 32.

[80] McMullen and Whelan, eds., *The Diary of Andrew Fuller*, 154.

[81] McMullen and Whelan, eds., *The Diary of Andrew Fuller*, 26.

similar to dementia, he found strength through contemplating Scripture. He recorded in his diary the following entry of July 25, 1792: "the afflictions in my family seem too heavy for me. I feel however some support from such Scriptures as these—All things shall work together for good &c. God, even our own God, shall bless us. It is of the Lord's mercy that I am not consumed.[82]

It was biblical meditation that brought peace and tranquility to Fuller's life. Fuller testified to the reality that the means by which he was able to engage in a greater walk with God was through meditation on scripture. For a busy period in Fuller's life he recorded little in his diary, but this entry of Friday, July 18, 1794, indicated the powerful way God was working in him as he meditated on Scripture:

> Within the last two years I have experienced perhaps as much peace and calmness of mind as at any former period. I have been enabled to walk somewhat more near to God than heretofore; and I find there is nothing that affords such preservation against sin—*if we walk in the Spirit, we shall not fulfill the lusts of the flesh*. This passage has been of great use to me ever since I preached from it … The sentiment on which I have principally discoursed was, that *Sin is not to be overcome so much by a direct or mere resistance of it, as by opposing other principles and considerations to it*. This Sentiment has been abundantly verified in my experience—So far as I have walked in the spirit, so far my life has been holy & happy—and I have experienced a good degree of these blessings compared with former times; though but a very small degree compared with what I ought to be.[83]

The entry above is a demonstration of how Fuller took a passage like Galatians 5 and allowed it to ruminate in his mind and then in his heart until eventually it resulted in a change in his life, a closer walk with God through the work of the Holy Spirit. Fuller exhorted those in his congregations as well as fellow pastors to engage in biblical meditation. However, before promoting this for others, his diary entries testify that he actively practiced this spiritual discipline personally in a way that brought great spiritual benefit.

### Biblical meditation of Andrew Fuller as described in selected sermons

In many of the sermons of Fuller we see the fruits of his practice of biblical meditation. Fuller in these sermons was concerned that he correctly understood and interpreted scripture and to facilitate this he was careful to observe

---

[82] McMullen and Whelan, eds., *The Diary of Andrew Fuller*, 184.

[83] McMullen and Whelan, eds., *The Diary of Andrew Fuller*, 186.

the larger context of the passages he preached on. In his approach to the text, he would ask a variety of questions of the text so that he might ponder things like contrast, and outcomes of the passages that he was interpreting. The meaning of the text he would then include in his sermon so that he could connect with the listeners minds. Yet, it was never enough to simply understand the bare meaning of the text that he expounded. It had to affect his heart and then the hearts of those attending to his message. Finally, Fuller would spend considerable time in trying to affect the will of his hearers through careful and pointed application. This process followed the classical practice of both the Puritans and the seventeenth-century Particular Baptists as they would also expound, explain the importance of a text, and then apply it to the hearts of the listeners.

Fuller gave a sermon on October 31, 1757, at the ordination of Robert Fawkner at Thorn, Bedfordshire.[84] The text was Acts 11:24, "He was good man, and full of the Holy Spirit, and of faith, and much people was added to the Lord." This good man was Barnabas. Before expounding the verse, Fuller made a point of looking at the larger context and especially examining all the other texts where Barnabas was mentioned. He points to three characteristics that the ordinand should emulate. The three points are those that clearly arose of out the text. As Fuller meditated on the text and the meaning became clear, he formulated his sermon based immediately from what was in the text, rather than imposing his own ideas upon it. Those three points were as follows. Barnabas was a good man, full of the Holy Spirit and faith. It is those three points Fuller developed, ending with the concept that evangelism was particularly blessed, expressed in the phrase "and much people were added to the Lord." Fuller made clear that it was the personal piety of Barnabas that directly contributed to the success that he had in ministry.[85] Fuller put it this way:

> I think it may be laid down as a rule, which both Scripture and experience confirm, that *eminent spirituality in a minister is usually attended with eminent usefulness.* I do not mean to say our usefulness depends on our spirituality, as an effect depends on its cause; nor yet that it is always in proportion to it. God is Sovereign and frequently sees proper to convince us of it, in variously bestowing his blessing on the means of grace. But yet he is not wanting in giving encouragement to what he approves, whenever it is found. Our want of usefulness is often to be ascribed to our want of spirituality, much oftener than to our want of talents.[86]

---

[84] Fuller, *Sermons and Sketches*, in *Works*, 1:135.

[85] Wheeler, "Eminent Spirituality," 190.

[86] Fuller, *Sermons and Sketches*, in *Works*, 1:143.

The means of grace that assist in becoming a good man, Fuller expounded in this sermon. One of these was to be active in "private retirements." Then Fuller referred to Paul's statement to Timothy "Meditate on those things, give yourself wholly to them."[87] Careful reading of the Bible and meditating upon it is critical for our personal spiritual growth, that we might be the "good man."[88]

On June 1, 1796, Fuller delivered *The Nature and Importance of an Intimate Knowledge of Divine Truth* before the Northamptonshire Association met at St. Albans. His text was Hebrews 5:12–16.[89] Describing the scriptures as the "oracles of God," Fuller stated:

> *We must learn truth immediately from the oracles of God.* Many religious people appear to be contented with seeing truth in the light in which some great and good man has placed it, but if ever we enter into the gospel purpose, it must be reading the word of God for ourselves, by praying and meditating upon its sacred contents. It is "in God's light that we must see light."[90]

Fuller indicated that one must receive God's truth directly from the Word. The means by which this was to be done was by reading it for oneself, meditating on that Word and combining that meditation with prayer. That is the proper way to discover the light of God's truth. Through sermons like this one, Fuller exhorted his hears to engage in the spiritual discipline of biblical meditation.

In a manner similar to the Puritans and seventeenth-century Calvinistic Baptists, Fuller suggested asking various questions of the text or topic under consideration. In this sermon he asked the question, "Would you contemplate the great *end of sin*?" He answered that question by indicating how a believer should view the topic of sin:

> You must view it in its connexions, tendencies, and consequences. For a poor finite creature, whose life is but a vapour, to gratify a vicious inclination may appear trifle, but when its tendencies and mischievous consequences are taken into the account, it wears a different aspect.[91]

By asking these questions regarding the end or result of sin, you enhance

---

[87] Fuller, *Sermons and Sketches*, in *Works*, 1:137.

[88] Fuller, *Sermons and Sketches*, in *Works*, 1:137.

[89] Fuller, *Sermons and Sketches*, in *Works*, 1:160.

[90] Fuller, *Sermons and Sketches*, in *Works*, 1:164.

[91] Fuller, *Sermons and Sketches*, in *Works*, 1:166.

your meditation upon the topic and begin to see it more fully. This is an example of the initial cognitive stage of meditation. Later in this sermon Fuller discusses contemplating the death of Christ and indicated that is possible to see in it only a suffering person in Jerusalem. We need to ask questions to probe deeper and grasp the greater truth. Initially after Christ's death the Apostles "minds were contracted, and sorrow filled their hearts."[92] Fuller stated further, "but when their eyes were opened to see it in is connexions and consequences, their sorrow was turned into joy."[93] Through asking questions as to the particular connections or consequences of a certain topic or text, one can probe and mine deeper truths. In this sermon, Fuller reminded his hearers to enhance continued growth in the knowledge of God and His word it was necessary to continually be in the Word:

> For in proportion as we love God, his word will *dwell richly in us*. It will be our bosom companion, to which we shall have recourse on every occasion, especially in season of leisure, when the mind, like a spring from which pressure is removed, rises to its natural position.[94]

Fuller made clear in this sermon that a simple reading of scripture to learn divine things was not enough. He wrote:

> To be contented with a superficial acquaintance with Divine thing implies also a want of affection for the things themselves … Nothing is more evident than that whatever is uppermost in our affections will form the grand current of our thoughts. And where our thoughts are directed to a subject with intenseness and perseverance, it will become familiar to us, and, unless it be owing to the want of natural capacity or any other necessary means, we shall of course enter deeply into it.[95]

Here Fuller made clear that careful thought and deep meditation were necessary to understand the truth of God and, moreover, this requires affection, a love for this truth. Fuller explained as well, that as believers persevere and focus deeply on a subject it will eventually reach deep within, to the affections. The end of meditation is not simply knowledge or even inflamed affections. As Fuller stated further in this sermon, "the word of God is represented as *a means*

---

[92] Fuller, *Sermons and Sketches*, in *Works*, 1:167.

[93] Fuller, *Sermons and Sketches*, in *Works*, 1:167.

[94] Fuller, *Sermons and Sketches*, in *Works*, 1:168.

[95] Fuller, *Sermons and Sketches*, in *Works*, 1:169.

*of sanctification."*[96] Fuller continued in the sermon to insist that we cannot simply bypass the mind and heart to affect the will. Biblical meditation requires that we understand first before the heart is affected and have the desires that will result in a change of our will. He stated:

> Now in order that the gospel may be productive of these effects, it is necessary that it be understood. Without this, how should it interest or affect the heart? We must *believe* the truth ere it will work effectively. We must *know* it or it will not make us free. That we serve God acceptably, with godly fear, we must have *grace*: and grace is multiplied "through the knowledge of God, and of Jesus our Lord" ... Knowledge and affection have a mutual influence on each other. That the love of truth will prompt us to labour after more perfect acquaintance with its contents has been already observed, and that such an acquaintance will promote an increasing love of truth, in return, is equally evident. We cannot love an unknown gospel, any more than an unknown God. Affection is fed by knowledge, being thereby furnished with grounds, or reasons for its operations. By the expansion of the mind the heart is supplied with objects which fill it with delight. It is thus that it becomes enlarged, and that we feel ourselves sweetly induced to "run in the way of Divine commandments."[97]

This representation is parallel to the understanding of biblical meditation and the tripartite nature of the human soul that was written about extensively by the Puritans and practiced by them and the seventeenth-century Reformed Baptists. First, we review the scriptures in our mind, turning the truths this way and that through a variety of questions. As we continue to contemplate the truths, they descend deeper and transform our affections so that our desires change, and we are now ready and willing to obey. Fuller continued to expound on this process by asking the question "How is it that the apostle became dead to the world by the cross of Christ? He answered: "I suppose, on much the same principle that the light of the stars is eclipsed by that of the sun ... It is by drinking deeply into religion that we become disaffected of carnal objects."[98]

Fuller continued to explain in this sermon how biblical meditation has great benefit to the Christian, because the Word of God is a source of enjoyment. Fuller put it this way:

---

[96] Fuller, *Sermons and Sketches*, in *Works*, 1:169.

[97] Fuller, *Sermons and Sketches*, in *Works*, 1:169.

[98] Fuller, *Sermons and Sketches*, in *Works*, 1:169–170.

The same way in which Divine truth operates as a medium of sanctification it becomes a source of enjoyment, namely, by interesting and affecting the heart. That which, by superior lustre, eclipses the pleasures of sense, and crucifies us to the world, at the same time kindles a joy in the heart which is unspeakable and full of glory. The habitual joy which was possessed by the apostles and primitive Christians chiefly arose from a knowledge and belief of the gospel.[99]

The pleasures of biblical meditation could be enjoyed at any time. Fuller knew that the Christian did not have to worry that they would not find in the scriptures good food to meditate on because he understood that "the Gospel is rich pasture."[100]

In a sermon that Fuller preached to a young minister at his ordination, *Spiritual Knowledge and Love Necessary for the Ministry*, Fuller described the main objects of ministry as, "you are aware that there are two main objects to be attained in the work of Christian ministry—*enlightening the minds* and *affecting the hearts* of the people."[101] Fuller was quick to add that this was only possible if the pastor was effective in this ministry. That effectiveness was dependent on whether the scripture and the truths that he would preach touched his life first. Fuller stated in many places that the way to have the Scripture impact us was to meditate upon it. He described the importance of being affected by biblical truths this way: "if you would enlighten others you must be under their influence. If you would enlighten others you must be 'a shining light' yourself. And if you would affect others, you yourself must feel, your own heart must 'burn' with holy ardour. You must be 'a *burning* and a *shining* light.'"[102]

In order to be effective in ministry Fuller told the young pastor:

You will need also, my brother, a heart *warmed* with Divine things, or you will never be "a burning and shining light." When we are thinking or preaching, we need to *burn*, as well as shine. When we study, we may race our brains, and form plans, but unless "our hearts burn within us," all will be a mere skeleton—our thoughts mere bones, whatever be their number, they will be all dry—very dry, and if we do not feel what we say, our preaching will be poor dead work.[103]

---

[99] Fuller, *Sermons and Sketches*, in *Works*, 1:170.

[100] Fuller, *Sermons and Sketches*, in *Works*, 1:478.

[101] Fuller, *Sermons and Sketches*, in *Works*, 1:478–479.

[102] Fuller, *Sermons and Sketches*, in *Works*, 1:479.

[103] Fuller, *Sermons and Sketches*, in *Works*, 1:480.

Fuller made clear that the ministry of enlightening minds and enflaming their hearts could not happen unless the preacher was first constantly feeding on the Word and having it burn to warm his affections. So, study and meditation of scripture in Fuller's mind was critical. At the end of his sermon to the young pastor Fuller gave this exhortation: *"study the word of God, above all other books, and pray over it. It is this will set our hearts on fire."*[104] The way to grow in understanding the scriptures and have it impact the heart is through biblical meditation. This is consistent and congruent with the understanding and practice of the Puritans and seventeenth-century Calvinistic Baptists.

Another sermon that Fuller preached that touches on biblical meditation was *On an Intimate and Practical Acquaintance with the Word of God*, which was on Ezra 7:10.[105] Fuller again stressed the importance of giving people knowledge of the Bible, but stressed that this could only be done if the pastor first possessed this knowledge himself. He argued, "you are to 'feed the people with knowledge and understanding,' but you cannot do this without understanding yourself. Your lips are to 'keep knowledge,' and the people are to 'seek the law at your mouth,' but, in order to communicate it to them you must seek it at the mouth of God."[106] In expounding on the phrase "seek the law of the Lord," Fuller urged: "*Seek it*, brother—It will never be found without. It is a mine, in which you have to dig. And it is a precious mine, which will well repay all your labour."[107] This digging would include meditation on scripture. Fuller insisted that this meant that a pastor needs to dig into the Word on his own, before consulting the opinions of others. So, he stated:

> Seek it *at the fountain-head*—You feel, I doubt not, a great esteem for many of your brethren now living, and admire the writings of some who are now no more; and you will read their productions with attention and pleasure. But whatever excellence your brethren possess, it is all borrowed, and it is mingled with error. Learn your religion from the Bible. Let that be your decisive rule. Adopt not a body of sentiments, or ever a single sentiment, solely on the authority of a man—however great, however respected. Dare to think for yourself.[108]

---

[104] Fuller, *Sermons and Sketches*, in *Works*, 1:481–482.

[105] Fuller, *Sermons and Sketches*, in *Works*, 1:483.

[106] Fuller, *Sermons and Sketches*, in *Works*, 1:483.

[107] Fuller, *Sermons and Sketches*, in *Works*, 1:483.

[108] Fuller, *Sermons and Sketches*, in *Works*, 1:483.

Next Fuller unpacked the phrase "prepare your heart to seek the law of the Lord." Concerning this preparation Fuller said, "It consists in prayer, and self-examination, and meditation."[109] He stated further, "Such preparation of heart is not only necessary for your *entrance* into the pastoral office, but also for your *continuance* in it. Let all your private meditations be mingled with prayer."[110] Fuller warned the candidate for ministry that biblical meditation and prayer should not be just for the purpose of preparing to speak to others, but that it is necessary that we feed our own soul first. He wrote, "Again, if we go to the Bible merely, or chiefly, to find something to say to the people without respect to our own souls, we shall make poor progress."[111] In a similar manner Fuller preached a sermon on Titus 2:15, and the phrase "Let no one despise thee."[112] This sermon was also directed to a pastor and Fuller gives the warning:

> *Beware that you do not preach an unfelt gospel*—If you do, it will be seen, and you will be despised. It will be seen that, though you affect to be in earnest, you do not feel; and that you scarcely believe your own doctrine. We may get into a habit of talking for the truth, and pleading for holiness, and yet be dead ourselves, and if so, se shall be sure to be despised.[113]

In another sermon, *Ministers Fellow Labourers with God*, Fuller instructed another pastor concerning the importance of meditating to help plumb the depths of scripture. He wrote:

> A leading part of this work consists in *our becoming acquainted with the mind of God in his word.*—We must "labour in word and doctrine." We cannot "feed the people with knowledge and with understanding," unless we possess them. Truth is a well—full of water, but deep. A depth is there in the word of God … Unless we labour in this way, there can be no proper food or variety in our preaching. "Meditate on these things give thyself wholly to them." … Digging in these mines is very pleasant work when we can enter into them. But there are seasons when it is otherwise; and yet we must go on, through we scarcely know how, this is *labour*.[114]

---

[109] Fuller, *Sermons and Sketches*, in *Works*, 1:484.

[110] Fuller, *Sermons and Sketches*, in *Works*, 1:484.

[111] Fuller, *Sermons and Sketches*, in *Works*, 1:484.

[112] Fuller, *Sermons and Sketches*, in *Works*, 1:489.

[113] Fuller, *Sermons and Sketches*, in *Works*, 1:489–490.

[114] Fuller, *Sermons and Sketches*, in *Works*, 1:492.

Fuller in this exhortation to a pastor declared that the primary work of a pastor is knowing the mind of God and passing on that truth to the people. The metaphors of a deep well to plummet and a mine to dig into, imply the challenge of the task. Biblical meditation is not always easy, but it reaps great benefits and it is a necessary discipline for the soul of the pastor and so that he might have a healthy spiritual diet of truth to feed the flock under his care.

When Fuller preached on the text of 1 Timothy 4:15-16, he focused on relation to one point of the sermon on the phrase, "take heed to thyself." He commented on that phrase with these words, "public religion, without that which is private and personal, is worse than no religion. We had better be anything than preachers of the gospel, unless we be personally interested in it."[115] Fuller in his ordination sermons continually challenged young pastors to make sure that they engaged in a vibrant private devotional life. For Fuller this was to include regular reading of scripture and then meditation on the Word, combined with prayer.

In his *Affectionate Concern of a Minister for the Salvation of his Hearers*, Fuller expounded on the text of 1 Thessalonians 2:7–8. He wrote of the necessity in our study and meditation on the gospel that we examine it through the asking of a variety of questions to help unpack the full meaning. He put it this way, "study the gospel—what it implies, what it includes, and what consequences it involves."[116] This is another example of how Fuller followed the practice of the Puritans and the seventeenth-century Particular Baptists in their approach to meditation of Scripture. In this sermon, Fuller spoke about the purpose of exhorting and encouraging obedience to the Scriptures. The Bible was written with the ability to produce this by affecting the heart and changing the desires. He wrote, "the doctrines of the Scriptures, Scripturally stated, are calculated to interest the heart, and to produce genuine evangelical obedience."[117]

The general structure of Fuller's sermons followed the pattern of the Puritans and Calvinistic Baptists of the seventeenth-century. He would begin with the exposition and explanation of a text, aimed at the human intellect. Then he would explain the doctrine that arose from the text and this was aimed at enflaming the heart. Finally, he would apply the truth to the specific context of his hearers with the desire to impact their will. An example of this can be found in a sermon entitled *The Reward of a Faithful Minister*, which focused on 1 Thessalonians 2:19.[118] In that sermon he wrote, "In discoursing on this interesting

---

[115] Fuller, *Sermons and Sketches*, in *Works*, 1:507.

[116] Fuller, *Sermons and Sketches*, in *Works*, 1:509.

[117] Fuller, *Sermons and Sketches*, in *Works*, 1:509

[118] Fuller, *Sermons and Sketches*, in *Works*, 1:542.

subject, I shall endeavor to explain it—account for it—and apply it."[119]

In an ordination sermon addressed to both the pastor and people of a congregation, Fuller expounded on the text of Galatians 5:13, "By love serve on another." The title of this message was *Ministers and Churches Exhorted to Serve One Another in Love*.[120] He addressed the pastor by exhorting him to be sure that he would serve the church "*by feeding them with the word of life.*"[121] He stated:

> For this end you must be familiar with the word. "Meditate on these things give thyself wholly to them." It is considered a fine thing with some to have a black coat, to loiter about all the week, and to stand up to be looked at and admired on the sabbath. But truly this is not to serve the church of God. Be concerned to be "a scribe *well instructed* in the things of the kingdom." Be concerned to have *treasures*, and bring them forth. I would advise that one service of every sabbath consist of a well-digested exposition, that your hearers may become Bible Christians.[122]

Here Fuller speaks again of the need for careful exposition, but that this exposition should be "well-digested" which implies that in the preparation the pastor has meditated thoroughly on the passage he will expound. So, biblical meditation for Fuller, was essential and beneficial first for the pastor's own soul, and then for the benefit of those who would hear him.

Another helpful sermon to consider was entitled, *Holding Fast the Gospel*. This was an exposition of 2 Timothy 1:13.[123] In following the pattern of traditional Reformed preaching, Fuller was concerned to follow the grammatical-historical approach in exegeting a text of Scripture. So, he began by addressing the context. He stated, "this Epistle was written on the near approach of death, and is very solemn. It is addressed to Timothy, and as such is doubtless especially applicable to minister, but by no means exclusively so, since all Scripture is given for the same of the church."[124] In a manner typical of most of Fuller's sermons, the outline of his sermon mirrors the main points within the text. For the first part of the message Fuller than expounded the meaning of the text, looking specifically at the meaning of the words. He explained what is

---

[119] Fuller, *Sermons and Sketches*, in *Works*, 1:542.

[120] Fuller, *Sermons and Sketches*, in *Works*, 1:544.

[121] Fuller, *Sermons and Sketches*, in *Works*, 1:544.

[122] Fuller, *Sermons and Sketches*, in *Works*, 1:544.

[123] Fuller, *Sermons and Sketches*, in *Works*, 1:547.

[124] Fuller, *Sermons and Sketches*, in *Works*, 1:547.

meant by "sound words" and then the "form" of sound words. He explains that the word "form" indicates that "it was only outline, only a sketch, for Timothy and all other Christians to fill up, and meditate upon. Paul did not know all. Angels do not. It will require eternity to know all. There is plenty of room for meditation, only let us keep within the lines which the apostles have sketched out."[125] Fuller again explains that scripture is something that ministers, and all Christians should regularly meditate upon, and that the scriptures provide a lifetime of material to engage. What the apostles have provided is the framework within which to meditate, the basic truths and theological tenets that form the outer fences of a spiritual garden, where we may taste all the produce through biblical meditation, while remaining within safe boundaries. Fuller examines the words "hold fast" next and to explain the text more completely, he gives examples of "contrast." He cites several examples of those who for various reasons do not hold fast to sound words. By employing the use of contrast, Fuller was able to unpack the text further to those who would hear him.

Fuller expounded the phrase "in faith and love" next. Here he explained the necessity of genuine faith that will be demonstrated in affection for the truth. He wrote:

> There is such a thing as a bigoted and blind attachment to doctrines, which will be of no use, even if they be true. The word does not profit, unless it be "mixed with faith." And there is such a thing as a sound creed, without charity, or love to God and men. But the gospel must be held in faith and love. The union of genuine orthodoxy and affection constitutes true religion.[126]

Fuller explained the text to engage the intellect and then he explained the importance of the truths in order to warm the heart. In the final section of this message Fuller presented several points of application in order to affect the will and exhort his hearers to an obedience response. He asked his hearers to consider the great value of the "sound words." Then, he reminded them how they are the only words that can meet the needs of "perishing sinners." He stated next "they are the *only source of a holy life*."[127] Finally, he explained that these sound words are "the *only source of real happiness*."[128] All these points of application were to encourage his hearers to engage in the word and to hold fast to the "sound words" of scripture.

---

[125] Fuller, *Sermons and Sketches*, in *Works*, 1:548.

[126] Fuller, *Sermons and Sketches*, in *Works*, 1:548–549.

[127] Fuller, *Sermons and Sketches*, in *Works*, 1:549.

[128] Fuller, *Sermons and Sketches*, in *Works*, 1:549.

Biblical meditation was a spiritual discipline that was of preeminent importance in the life of Andrew Fuller. His high view of scripture created the need to engage the Bible with diligence to understand it as deeply as possible. Fuller followed the pattern of biblical meditation that Puritans and Calvinistic Baptists of the seventeenth-century employed. He began by examining the context of a passage, the grammar and meaning of words with the goal of understanding the text. Fuller would then ask questions of the text to probe deeper, followed by asking himself questions so that he might awaken and ignite his affections. Finally, Fuller would consider in very practical terms, the proper responses to the truths of the text, so that he might be obedient to the Word of God. The commitment that Fuller had to this process of biblical meditation is evident in the personal record of his diary and in many of his sermons. For Fuller, the Christian and lay person alike, must understand the word, so that their heart might be warmed in a deeper love for Christ, resulting in a joyful and willing obedience. The spiritual discipline that gave considerable facilitation towards this was biblical meditation.

Texts & documents

# Three Prayers from John Collett Ryland, *Introduction to the Knowledge of the Holy Spirit*

Introduced by Garrett Walden and selected by Michael A.G. Haykin

Garrett Walden is a PhD student in historical and theological studies at The Southern Baptist Theological Seminary, and a pastor at Grace Heritage Church in Auburn, Alabama.

Michael A.G. Haykin is chair and professor of Church History, The Southern Baptist Theological Seminary, Louisville, KY.

---

*Introduction*

John Collett Ryland (1723–1792) pastored two influential Particular Baptist churches in the English Midlands: at Warwick (1746–1759) and at Northampton (1759–1785). His final years were spent in Enfield, near London (1786–1792). In each of these three locales he led successful boarding schools for boys, earning him an international reputation as an educator. His dual vocation as a pastor and schoolmaster provided him the occasion to produce a few dozen books and pamphlets on topics ranging from theology and history to linguistics and the natural sciences.

In my effort to compile an exhaustive bibliography of Ryland's writings, a title appeared within Ryland's extant works which I could not locate: *Contemplations on the Divinity of the Holy Spirit; the Beauties of Creation, and Providence.*

*of Regeneration, Sanctification, or Vital Holiness; and Final Perseverance in Grace.* This title, with a detailed outline, was proposed for subscriptions at the end of his *Contemplations on the Divinity of Christ* (1782).[1] Two years later it was proposed for subscriptions again under the same title at the end of his *A Sermon Occasioned by the Death of the Rev. Andrew Gifford, D.D.* (1784), with the comment that "the manuscript has been preparing for many years," but that there were not yet enough subscribers to merit an uninterrupted print run.[2] This work then seemed to disappear.

I tried in vain to locate this work by the proposed title and had resolved that it likely was never produced, or shelved in an archive in England, or even lost through the years. However, in reviewing an entry in the January 1792 edition of *The Christian's Magazine* (the entry appears to be by William Newman, Ryland's teaching assistant in Enfield, as it is signed "W.N."), I discovered a similar title explicitly linked to "Mr. Ryland, senior" as the author.[3] I believe this is the work for which I had been searching (or at least a version of it). The full published title is *An Introduction to the Knowledge of the Holy Spirit, as a Divine Person in the Undivided Being of God, with a View of His Works of Creation, Inspiration and Miracles, Regeneration and Perseverance, and the Resurrection of the Dead, with the Worship Due to Him in the Churches of Christ.*[4] It is formally anonymous, but the Newman's magazine entry confirms the treatise as Ryland's.

This treatise is fascinating on numerous counts, not just for its orthodox and classical pneumatology, but also for the devotional asides and seraphic bursts of doxology typical of Ryland's writing. Further, this work contains material that deepens our understanding of Ryland as a theologian and assists in developing a more holistic view of his thought. Finally, his writing on the latter-day glory in this treatise confirms a remark made by John Ryland Jr., in his memoir of Andrew Fuller, when he states that his father's eschatology was in lock-step with that of John Gill. Prior to my discovery of this treatise, I had been unable

---

[1] John Ryland, *Contemplations on the Divinity of Christ, Evinced from His Names Jehovah, God, and Sovereign Lord; His Attributes and Actions; the Beauties of Creation, Providence, and Redemption; and the Acts of Worship Paid to Him in Scripture* (London: Thomas Dicey and Co., 1782).

[2] *A Sermon Occasioned by the Death of the Rev. Andrew Gifford, D.D., by John Rippon ... with An Address Delivered at His Interment, by the Rev. John Ryland, A.M.*, 2nd ed. (London: T. Wilkins, 1784).

[3] W[illiam] N[ewman], "Select Books," *The Christian's Magazine* 3 (1792): 34.

[4] [John Collett Ryland], *An Introduction to the Knowledge of the Holy Spirit, as a Divine Person in the Undivided Being of God, with a View of His Works of Creation, Inspiration and Miracles, Regeneration and Perseverance, and the Resurrection of the Dead, with the Worship Due to Him in the Churches of Christ* (London: Thomas Wilkins, 1786).

to corroborate Ryland Jr.'s note within Ryland Sr.'s own corpus.[5]

What follows are three prayers from this hitherto unknown work by Ryland that have been selected by the editor of this journal that illustrate not only Ryland, Sr.'s piety, but also provide a window upon the spirituality of the Particular Baptists during the eighteenth century.

Text

*Prayers to the Holy Spirit* by John Collett Ryland

"O! eternal Jehovah the Holy Spirit, we love thee with supreme esteem rising into veneration. We rise higher still into the most awful adoration of thy perfections. We admire all thy works of creation and providence, of revelation and grace. We would feel the highest gratitude for all thy rich and various blessings of nature and salvation. We long to make the best returns of love and joy; we wish for higher powers, and then we will be more grateful. We love ourselves when we feel the warmest gratitude; and we abhor ourselves when we feel our hearts unthankful; and in thy strength we will be more and more grateful, as long as life and thought and immortality endures."[6]

"We do adore thee, O divine Spirit of wisdom and love. We consecrate all our powers to thy sovereign pleasure. We subject our conscience and will to thy holy will. We do bitterly repent that we have ever affronted and grieved thee. We feel an unbounded delight in thy beauty and grace. We have an eager desire to see thy glory displayed as bright as ten thousand suns and are grieved

---

[5] See the comment in John Ryland Jr., *The Work of Faith, the Labour of Love, and the Patience of Hope, illustrated; in the Life and Death of the Rev. Andrew Fuller, Late Pastor of the Baptist Church at Kettering, and Secretary to the Baptist Missionary Society, from its Commencement, in 1792*, 2nd ed. (London: Button & Son, 1818), 112, n.*, where the younger Ryland writes about his father:

> It is true, he admitted the idea of a personal reign of Christ upon the earth, between the first and second resurrection, in which he followed Dr. Gill, and supposed that this period is properly to be stiled the Millennium: but he also expected that long before this the gospel would be spread all over the world, and the fulness of the Jews and of the Gentiles be brought into the church; and I never remember his expressing an expectation of miraculous gifts being granted for that end. … I do not see how their opinion, whether it be right or wrong, could prove any impediment to exertion for spreading the gospel. What they denominated the latter-day glory, or the spiritual reign of Christ, would be none the less desirable, nor less the object of exertion, on account of its being followed by his personal reign, after the first resurrection.

Compare Ryland Sr., *Introduction to the Knowledge of the Holy Spirit*, 104, with John Gill, "The Watchman's Answer to the Question: What of the Night?," in his *A Collection of Sermons and Tracts* (London: George Keith, 1773), 1:28; and Barry Howson's explanation of Gill's eschatology in his "The Eschatology of the Calvinistic Baptist John Gill (1697–1771) Examined and Compared," *Eusebeia* 5 (Autumn 2005): 33–66.

[6] Ryland Sr., *Introduction to the Knowledge of the Holy Spirit*, 44. The punctuation has been modernized.

to see thee dishonoured by thy wicked and malicious enemies. And we love to give the highest praise to thy divine and immortal majesty, world without end. Let the whole creation praise thee, for all nature is thy temple, all space is thine abode, all angels are thy production, all believers are thy peculiar habitation. Let therefore all Christian preachers and people cry out every hour *Halleluia*! the Lord God omnipotent the blessed Spirit reigneth; and may [praise to] God the Father and the Son resound through heaven and earth, Amen and Amen."[7]

"O divine and eternal Spirit, come into our hearts, enlighten our minds, renew our will, purge our affections, pacify our consciences, strengthen our weak memories, refine and elevate our taste, sanctify our imaginations, fix our attention on God and things invisible, make Christ infinitely precious to our faith and love, display in the most lively manner, and in the brightest light, all the rich and powerful motives of the gospel; and give us an inward strength and bent of mind to comply with those motives to the very uttermost of our power and with the greatest cheerfulness, joy and pleasure, all through life! This, this is the whole of our desires, this is the sum total of all our wishesand hopes in life and death. Amen."[8]

---

[7] Ryland, *Introduction to the Knowledge of the Holy Spirit*, 80–81. The punctuation has been modernized.

[8] Ryland, *Introduction to the Knowledge of the Holy Spirit*, 119. The spelling and punctuation have been modernized.

# James Hinton on the assurance of the Father's love

Edited and introduced by Chance Faulkner

Chance Faulkner serves as a Junior Fellow of the Andrew Fuller Center for Baptist Studies and is a MTh candidate at Union School of Theology in Wales.

---

*Introduction*
One of the inescapable realities of every believer is that of indwelling sin. Though the penalty of our sin has been dealt with in Christ, until glory the lingering reality of sin remains. Old sins pop its head up once again, and new sins emerge. And like our first parents, our temptation is to run away and hide among the fig leaves of our shame.

In this heartwarming letter, James Hinton (1761–1823) encourages his daughter struggling with the assurance of her salvation.[1] Affectionately, pastorally, and fatherly, Hinton points her to the only cure for her guilt. The solution to her shame of indwelling sin is to see a fresh picture of the Father heart of God—the never-ending, overflowing abundance of love. Nothing good she does will cause the Father to love her more, and no failure will cause the Father to love her less. For the benevolence and loving kindness of the Father far outweighs her sin. Hinton exhorts her to look to Christ the Son—the friend of sinners who "is ever present with you, sees every thought of your heart, and listens with infinite delight." The most honourable thing she can do is to lean her full weight upon Christ: to flee to him for refuge in his perfect righteousness

---

[1] Hinton had two daughters: Sarah Hinton (1796–1813) and Ann (Neé Hinton) Bartlett (1795–1866). For Hinton's letter to Ann on her marriage see, Chance Faulkner, ed., "'You will scarcely need another intimate friend': A letter of James Hinton to his daughter, Ann, on her marriage," *JAFS* 4 (February 2022): 65–79.

and sufficient work as Mediator, and trust that, in him, she is fully welcomed into the privileges of a child of God and co-heir with Christ.

This letter sheds light on Hinton as a father and reveals his relationship with his own children: affectionate, compassionate, loving, kind, and eager to see Christ formed in them. But it also demonstrates what Hinton believed to be at the heart of Christian growth: it is by meditating and going deeper into the free and pardoning love of God in Christ that "the heart [is] melted, the tempter defeated, and the soul ... comforted and sanctified."

Though this was penned over two hundred years ago, is this not the temptation of every believer in every age? Time and time again, our sin causes us to be suspicious of our assurance before God the Father. But time and time again, God the Father surprises us with his unwavering loving-kindness, with his unconditional and lavishing grace. Though indwelling sin is an inescapable reality for the believer now, our great hope is in the assurance that in Christ, we share in his status, and so we have the privilege, through the Spirit, of crying, "Abba, Father."

*Text*

Why is it, my dear child, that you, who doubt not a moment of your earthly father's love, should hesitate to believe the precious promises which assure you of that of your heavenly Father? But you say, you "have never offended the former as you have the latter" ... I allow there is no comparison in the degree of offence; but neither is there any, as you well know, in the degree of benevolence and love. His love is without degree—it cannot be equalled even by human guilt; and this, if anything could, must have accomplished the task. The sea of mercy "hath neither shore nor bound."[2] Behold that dear, that exalted, that condescending Friend of sinners, whom you can never please so well as by giving the fullest credit to his assurance that he is your Friend, your Redeemer, your guide through earth, your portion forever. What a mercy that you have lived to know that such a glorious person exists, is ever present with you, sees every thought of your heart, and listens with infinite delight to every sigh which says, "O that he were mine!" What a blessing that you have lived to see and feel your need of such a friend!

Do not offend him by distrusting him. I know what your views of the human heart are. I had the same at your age, and was overwhelmed by them;[3] but believe me, my dear girl, to accept freely the pardoning mercy of God, to listen to the voice: "Daughter, be of good cheer, thy sins are forgiven thee"—this is the

---

[2] Isaac Watts, stanza 5 of "Sufficiency of Pardon," *Hymns and Spiritual Songs* (London, 1707), 158.

[3] See John Howard Hinton, *A Biographical Portraiture of the Late Rev. James Hinton, M.A., Pastor of a Congregational Church in the City of Oxford* (Oxford: Bartlett and Hinton; London: B.J. Holdsworth, 1824), 9–12.

only way to have the heart melted, the tempter defeated, and the soul at once comforted and sanctified.[4] Approach, dear child, and touch the sceptre.[5] You cannot render to God a service so pleasing, so acceptable, so honourable to his nature and word, as to put away all your objections on account of sinful nature, hardness of heart, proneness to forget God, and all other complaints, and say, "Notwithstanding all these—nay, induced by them all—I flee for refuge to the perfect atonement and righteousness of the Lord Jesus. By him, blessed Mediator I am assured that God will put away all my guilt, that I shall be admitted, with a full welcome, to all the privileges of the children of God, and heirs of glory."

"What, though I am such a sinful creature?" Yes, my child, though you were a thousand times worse, it would not prevent your acceptance nor your salvation. You do not think that a father would deceive. On this hope I rest my eternal all. Come, share with me the blessing, and you shall be happy. I do not say, you will be always in a happy frame; but resting on divine truth, you will be always safe. Joyful when in the light, patient and humble when in the dark; but always in the way to Zion, and sure to arrive there at last.

---

[4] Matthew 9:22.

[5] See Esther 4:11.

# "Of the future happiness of infants I have no doubt:" James Hinton on the death of a child

Edited and introduced by Chance Faulkner

Chance Faulkner serves as a Junior Fellow of the Andrew Fuller Center for Baptist Studies and is an MTh candidate at Union School of Theology in Wales.

*Introduction*
One the key differences between the long eighteenth century and our day is the devastating reality of child mortality during the former. For instance, in the first decade of the nineteenth century, one out of three children did not live to see their fifth birthday.[1] For someone living in the twenty-first century in the West, this is a difficult statistic to comprehend. The advancement of medical training and technology gives us the reasonable assumption our children will be born healthy and live to old age. While there are exceptions, this is the reality in which we live and move: few parents will experience the deaths of their children in infancy. But for those who came before us, the potential death of their infant children would have been a constant fear.[2]

Christians believe in the fallen nature of the human heart from conception, and thus all deserve condemnation. Yet every parent who has experienced the

---

[1] This percentage is based on child mortality in London. See Peter Razzell and Christine Spence, "The History of Infant, Child and Adult Mortality in London, 1550–1850," *The London Journal* 32, No. 3 (2007): 273.

[2] Andrew Fuller (1754–1815), for example, lost nine out of fourteen or fifteen children in infancy.

death of a child is forced to ask: What about my child? Are they morally accountable? Will they be damned? Does the Bible warrant any hope or assurance for them? James Hinton (1761–1823) seemed to think so.

In the following letter, Hinton sought to provide comfort and assurance for a mother, likely one of the members of his Particular Baptist church in Oxford, who was bereaved of her son. Hinton had every assurance of her child's happiness in heaven. He based his reasoning upon two main passages: Matthew 19:14 (cf. Mark 10:14; Luke 18:16), and 2 Samuel 12:23. He also reasoned from the God's supreme goodness. The God who "waits with much long suffering on sinners who wilfully spend many years in rebellion," he argued, will certainly secure the future happiness of those "who can never be conscious of having once wilfully offended his holy Majesty."

Hinton also touched upon the concept of what is called the age of accountability.[3] Though wary of claiming such assurance for anyone above ten, yet he admitted, "At what hour, or in what year, of life, moral accountability commences, or to what extent at first it reaches, the blessed God ... has not revealed to us."

Hinton and his wife Ann experienced the loss of a one-year-old son to measles in 1793, so his encouragement was from one who had drunk from the same cup of affliction and on a topic he had obviously thought deeply about.[4]

---

[3] Christopher Anderson (1782–1852), the Scottish Baptist, writing to Andrew Fuller on the death of his nine-year-old niece, says that she was in "a most interesting period of life for a child to die," though he was assured that she bore "the evidence [of saving faith] such as is scarcely to be found in infant years" (Hugh Anderson, *The Life and Letters of Christopher Anderson* [Edinburgh: William P. Kennedy; London: Hamilton Adams, and Co., n.d], 158–160). As noted above, Fuller himself had experienced significant loss as well. One particular loss was a six-year-old girl, "of whose Christianity" he said, "I had considerable hopes" (Anderson, *Life and Letters of Christopher Anderson*, 160). Fuller and Anderson did not seem to have the same assurance as Hinton had, though the line "a most interesting period of life for a child to die" might imply a recognition of the concept of age of accountability which Hinton is suggesting.

A few decades later, C.H. Spurgeon (1834–1892), the famous Baptist Preacher and a self-proclaimed "Fullerite," was bold enough to say "I have never, at any time in my life, said, believed, or imagined that any infant, under any circumstances, would be cast into hell ... I do not believe that, on this earth, there is a single professing Christian holding the damnation of infants; or, if there be, he must be insane, or utterly ignorant of Christianity." (Letter to [a Correspondent], June 12, 1869, in *The Letters of Charles Spurgeon* [London; New York: Marshall Brothers, 1923], 215). According to the Second London Confession of Faith, 10.3, "Elect infants dying in infancy are regenerated and saved by Christ through the Spirit; who worketh when, and where, and how he pleases; so also are all elect persons, who are incapable of being outwardly called by the ministry of the Word."

[4] John Howard Hinton, *A Biographical Portraiture of the Late Rev. James Hinton, M.A., Pastor of a Congregational Church in the City of Oxford* (Oxford: Bartlett and Hinton; London: B.J. Holdsworth, 1824), 52, 72.

*Text*
My dear friend,

To comfort those who are cast down is the work of a divine hand, but that of a fellow Christian is often employed as the means of communication. Of the future happiness of infants I have no doubt. Our Lord, in saying, "Of such is the kingdom of God," certainly meant to comfort the parents by this assurance, as well as to teach them humility and simplicity of character.[5] And thus David comforted himself when he said of his infant child, "I shall go to him, though he shall not return to me."[6] It is, moreover, entirely inconsistent with all our ideas of divine goodness, to believe that he who waits with much long suffering on sinners who wilfully spend many years in rebellion, should at once plunge into endless woe millions of millions of infant beings, who can never be conscious of having once wilfully offended his holy Majesty. To all who die in this morally unconscious state, I believe that the second Adam restored the ruins of the first. They die because Adam sinned; they live because Jesus died. So far I have no fear on this head.

At what hour, or in what year, of life, moral accountability commences, or to what extent at first it reaches, the blessed God (doubtless for wise and good ends) has not revealed to us. Had your dear boy been ten, or twelve, or fourteen years of age, my anxiety would have been much greater than it is; but, I confess, were I in your place, I should have no distressing fear on the dear child's account. The reasons I have already stated apply very forcibly to his case; and, if any doubt remains, it is in a great measure done away by the very pleasing account which you give, of his having conversed feelingly upon death and eternity, and of his saying eagerly, "O yes!" when he was asked "if he should love to go to heaven, and dwell with Christ." My feelings as a parent would be full of hope that he is "forever with the Lord."[7] With this we must rest satisfied; since if the blessed God were to give us full certainty, it might lead to pernicious complacency in the state of those who live, and check those strenuous exertions which he has appointed as means for their salvation; means which he gave you a heart to use, and on which (as far as the case admits) he gave proofs of his blessing.

---

[5] Matthew 19:14; Mark 10:14; Luke 18:16.

[6] 2 Samuel 12:23.

[7] 1 Thessalonians 4:17.

*The Journal of Andrew Fuller Studies*
5 | September 2022

# Joseph Kinghorn's pedagogical advice to William Newman

## Edited by Baiyu Andrew Song

Baiyu Andrew Song FRAS is the assistant professor of general education studies at Heritage College and Seminary, Cambridge, ON, and an adjunct lecturer at Redeemer University, Ancaster, ON.

---

## Introduction

Twice in the early 1800s, Joseph Kinghorn was offered the principalship of newly-founded Baptist academies—Northern Academy (1804) and Stepney Academy (1809).[1] However, the Norwich minister did not accept the invitations from either Yorkshire or London. In his letters to Joseph Gutteridge (1752–1844), Kinghorn explained to the Baptist merchant and the committee members of London Baptist Educational Fund that "if it be [God's] will that

---

[1] On the Northern Academy, see Thomas Steadman, *Memoir of the Rev. William Steadman, D.D.* (London: Ward and Co., 1838); Peter Shepherd, *The Making of a Northern Baptist College* ([Manchester]: Northern Baptist College, 2004); Anthony R. Cross, *Useful Learning: Neglected Means of Grace in the Reception of the Evangelical Revival among English Particular Baptists* (Eugene, OR: Pickwick, 2017), 225–234; Michael A.G. Haykin, "'With light, beauty, and power': Educating English Baptists in the Long Eighteenth Century," in *Challenge and Change: English Baptist Life in the Eighteenth Century*, edited by Stephen L. Copson and Peter J. Morden (Didcot, Oxfordshire: Baptist Historical Society, 2017), 195–197. On Stepney Academy, see R.E. Cooper, *From Stepney to St. Giles': The Story of Regent's Park College, 1810–1960* (London: Carey Kingsgate, 1960); Cross, *Useful Learning*, 409–412; Haykin, "With light, beauty, and power," 191–194; Anthony J. Clarke, and Paul S. Fiddes, *Dissenting Spirit: A History of Regent's Park College, 1752–2017* (Oxford: Centre for Baptist History and Heritage Studies, Regent's Park College, 2017).

I should now leave Norwich and come to London, it is on a plan materially different from that by which he has hitherto guided me."[2] For Kinghorn, the primary reason to reject Gutteridge's invitation to lead Stepney Academy was his pastoral calling at St. Mary's in Norwich. Nevertheless, when Gutteridge wrote to Kinghorn, a number of key events had happened in Norwich. In 1810, Kinghorn's parents David (1737–1822) and Elizabeth Kinghorn (1737/8–1810) had already moved to live with their son for ten years, and later that same year, Elizabeth died after being ill for a long period of time. Since his father's unhappy dismissal at Bishop Burton in 1799, Kinghorn had promised his parents to take care of them.[3] Furthermore, as Kinghorn explained to Gutteridge, the St. Mary's congregation experienced unseen growth under Kinghorn's pastorate, for which the congregation decided to build a new and enlarged building on the same site.[4] Kinghorn thus had no reason to move. Though the Baptists in London missed the opportunity to have a respective pastor-scholar to be the first principal of Stepney Academy, they were glad to secure William Newman (1773–1835)—with Andrew Fuller's (1754–1815) recommendation—to lead the new school.[5] Therefore, at a meeting on November 27, 1810, the London committee resolved unanimously to invite Newman to "undertake the office of Resident Tutor" at Stepney.[6] On March 25, 1811, Newman, his family, and six of his pupils moved from Bromley to Stepney.

It seems that Newman was anxious about his new post, though he had been a private tutor for many years. In early 1811, Newman sent letters to a number

---

[2] Joseph Kinghorn to Joseph Gutteridge, May 23, 1810, in Edward Steane, *Memoir of the Life of Joseph Gutteridge, Esq. of Denmark Hill, Surrey* (London: Jackson and Walford, 1850), 101.

[3] After twenty-eight years of ministry, David Kinghorn and the Bishop Burton congregation were involved in an irreconcilable dispute over church discipline. As David Kinghorn explained to the Particular Baptist Fund, the quarrel began with his public reproof of Jane Ross (1743–1816), the wife of Simon Gregson (1739–1817), who was one of the deacons (David Kinghorn to Benjamin Tomkins, November 16, 1799, D/KIN 2/1799 no. 996 [Angus Library and Archive, Regent's Park College, Oxford], 1). This dispute physically impacted David Kinghorn. Through his letters, Joseph Kinghorn comforted his father and suggested that his parents relocate to Norwich to live with him. In one of his letters, Joseph Kinghorn assured his aging parents that he was financially able to support them (Joseph Kinghorn to David Kinghorn, January 31, 1799, D/KIN 2/1799 no. 975 [Angus Library and Archive, Regent's Park College, Oxford]).

[4] Steane, *Memoir of the Life of Joseph Gutteridge*, 98. In February 1811, the congregation collected a total of £3,650 for the new building, and in March 1811, Kinghorn laid the foundation for the new chapel. See C.B. Jewson, "St. Mary's, Norwich, V," *Baptist Quarterly* 10.6 (1941): 343–344.

[5] Regarding Kinghorn, Gutteridge wrote: "the friends in London are not altogether strangers to your probity of character, your literary attainments, nor to the interest you take in instructing young men for the work of the ministry; and above all, to your sincere regard to personal piety" (Steane, *Memoir of the Life of Joseph Gutteridge*, 79). On Newman, see George Pritchard, *Memoir of the Rev. William Newman, D.D.* (London: Thomas Ward and Co., 1837), 231–233.

[6] Pritchard, *Memoir of the Rev. William Newman*, 233.

of Baptist ministers requesting advice for the institution and curriculum. It seems that Kinghorn's letter was the most extensive one, though Newman did not mention receiving a letter from Kinghorn in his diary. Regarding the letter, it is interesting to observe that one of Kinghorn's primary concerns was about the new academy's graduates, as many graduates of other dissenting academies became Arians or Socinians upon graduation. As early as 1796, Kinghorn told his parents about a conversation with a Socinian clergyman, who told Kinghorn that "Socinian principles on the Char[acter] of Christ did not arise from the plain language of Revelation—but there was no defending nor understanding Christianity if we did not put such an interpretation upon it."[7] Furthermore, according to Kinghorn, "the true reason why the new College at Hackney fell was many of the young men training for the pulpit went into Deism."[8] Thus, beside the zeitgeist of the age, the dissenting academies also contributed to the widespread of Socinianism. Kinghorn, therefore, provided a plan for reforming the academies in his letter to the new principal, as he believed that by the plan he laid out, many could avoid turning away from Christian orthodoxy, and the school could train men of godliness for the ministry.

*Notes on the Text*
Though Martin Hood Wilkin (1832–1904) transcribed and included parts of this long letter in his biography, Wilkin's extract was selective and deconstructive.[9] In Wilkin's biography, he re-ordered the paragraphs by taking the first two paragraphs from a latter part of the letter and made them the opening paragraphs. It was, however, fortunate that the entire letter was preserved by Wilkin and later by C.B. Jewson (1909–1981), as the two-folio-long letter is now collected in the [Simon] Wilkin Papers in Norfolk Record Office. The following transcription seeks preserve the original layout of Kinghorn's letter. All spellings are original, except indicated.
*Text*[10]

---

[7] Joseph Kinghorn to David Kinghorn, July 5, 1796, D/KIN 2/1796 no. 877 (Angus Library and Archive, Regent's Park College, Oxford), 1.

[8] Joseph Kinghorn to David Kinghorn, July 5, 1796, D/KIN 2/1796 no. 877 (Angus Library and Archive, Regent's Park College, Oxford), 1. New College, Hackney, or Hackney College was based at Dr. Williams's Library in Cripplegate from 1786 to 1796. Though it was founded by the London Presbyterian Fund as a non-denominational academy, the school was biased towards Unitarianism. Many well-known Socinians were associated with the school. See Thomas Belsham, *Knowledge the Foundation of Virtue: A Sermon Addressed to the Young Persons who Attended the Gravel Pit Meeting, Hackney* (London, 1795); Belsham, *Memoirs of the Late Theophilus Lindesey* (London, 1812); H.W. Stephenson, *William Hazlitt and Hackney College* (London: Lindsey, 1930).

[9] Martin Hood Wilkin, *Joseph Kinghorn, of Norwich* (Norwich: Fletcher and Alexander, 1855), 334–338.

[10] Joseph Kinghorn to William Newman, March 13, 1811, #36, Wilkin Papers, MC64/12, 508X8 (Nor-

Dear Sir [1]
Various things have prevented my sending you the promised
letter, you will find it now my miscellaneous. Perhaps I shall omit the vary
things you wished I should notice, & state my opinion on others concerning
which your mind is made up. Be it as it may, if any remarks now made are [5]
useful to you I shall rejoice; If you imagine that or any other subjects
I can render you a service, let me know.
The first thing which will strike you & the Committee, ~~are of~~ will be the
only goodness
selection of Students. This is of the greatest importance. And ^ the ^ ~~care~~ of
God can ~~above~~ prevent you from bring greatly deceived. A truly serious spirit in [10]
the students is of the greatest consequence. If they really know the Grace of
God in truth, it will bring them sound after a variety of difficulties to the
right place. This is so essential that our Churches as well as Tutors, should
endeavour to keep their eyes always upon it. It has often been a subject
of complaint, that our Academies do not contribute to the preservation [15]
of the seriousness of the Students. A number of young men meeting
on an equality—few from anxiety respecting this present support
living together at a time of life when the spirits are high—and, who
after their studies feel their minds relax ~~with~~ in proportion to their former
tension, are prone to forget themselves. It is too much to expect that [20]
this will not be the case. There is a tendency to Levity—to Criticism
—and to all the playfulness of mind to which their natural character
induce them. They are apt to be lavish in their conversation,—to urge
each other or in speculation, & these go lengths they never thought of.
When their views begin to expand, they imagine they either do, or can [25]
comprehend every thing attainable by man;—and often despise both
books & men which they afterwards revere. They are apt to imagine
that what is plain is worth nothing, & are seeking continually for something

[p. 2]
original, & ~~have~~ they will often reject what they ought to embrace. [1]
Hence will arise your most arduous labor! And I think not how you
can better assist your pupils to escape, the worst part at least of these
evils, than by your earnest prayers—your frequent exhortation—&
your affectionate counsel. Endeavour to impress
upon them the importance [5]
of cultivating personal Godliness. Show them their need of Humility.—Hold

folk Record Office, Norwich).

up to their view the end for which they come into you house, & the objects which will engage them after they have left it. Most of them must relive into situations of comparative obscurity, in which much will depend on their seriousness—their zeal—their humility & their prudence. They will often [10] need patience, & ^must exercise^ self denial, when they come into actual service. Their sentiments—their a~~q~~cquaintance with experimental religion—their manners—their general deportment—their dress—their every thing, will be narrowly watched both by friends & foes. It should therefore be their study to cultivate the train of thinking & the habits ^which^ they will afterwards need, [15] as well as to apply to their books, otherwise the labour of <u>unlearning</u> many things will be as great, as that of <u>learning</u> any thing you may teach. To commit serious errors, which will hurt the pious part of a Congregation, and open the mouths of the giddy & irreligious is easy;—to repair them is difficult. [20]
You will prevent many evils, by making the Students a part of your family, & living considerably with them. This will keep order, & check many follies which would take place at Meals. You will do well also to pay particular attention to your family worship. Not so much respecting its length, as that it is regular & performed in a [25] manner likely to support devotional feeling. Let it not be broken in upon, or treated as an affair of mere conveniency.
A considerable practical difficulty will arise respecting instruction in Divinity. If you take any usual plan objections will be raised against it.

[p. 3]
One will be called inefficient, another will ~~lay~~ put fetters on the mind [1] & cramp free enquiry &c. Some have thought instructions on these subjects best vivâ voce. After all you must have some plan in your mind, & you must follow it with regularity. Perhaps the following might be worth trying. Suppose you require a thesis [5] or sermon from 2 or 3 Students (to be delivered on such a day) on some important part of the Christian Religion. These would furnish some for remarks, had you to state your view of the subject, in its nature—evidence—& importance;—you would also introduce such illustrations as the subject required. Then direct that a [10] thesis or sermon be produced by 2 or 3 others on another given subject ~~against~~ ^on^ another day. By this means you would exercise their minds, & had them to seek such information as they might need.

Thus under your direction the most important parts of Christianity
would pass under review in less time than one would suppose, [15]
I should hesitate about adopting the plan of reading Lectures on
Divinity, if I were in your situation. But you must have an
outline of your own which will gradually enlarge & improve.
The prejudice against a regular course of Instruction in divinity, I know
is great, & the outcry against it as Systematic, is too popular.[11] But is [20]
foolish to imagine, that religion is the only thing in which arrangement
does nothing;—or that young men who may be capable of preaching
an acceptable plain sermon, know every thing in divinity by intuition,
and have the privilege of despising whatever may be nick-named
a System. Too much of this folly however does exist. [25]

[p. 4]
That which will render it necessary to adopt some regular plan of [1]
explaining and discussing the leading points of the Christian Doctrine, is, that
you will find young men sent to you, who will hear of some of them for
the first time in your house. Many very useful ministers are on such
narrow ground, that they never fairly to their proper extent state, a variety [5]
of things which have a place in the Christian System; and of course such
young men as arise from their Churches are in a very uninformed state
condition. These will be particularly benefitted by your instruction, if

---

[11] According to W.R. Ward (1925-2010), due to the common assumptions of the Enlightenment, eighteenth-century evangelicals adopted "the metaphysical approach to theology," and they applied "the inductive method in the field of religion, while the polemical backwoodsmen were sacrificing the truth to system" (Ward, *Religion and Society in England 1790-1850* [London: B.T. Batsford, 1972], 17). Therefore, for them, "it was system, … which seemed to account for the unhappy embarrassments of the past, especially in regard to reprobation, and high and low, 'system' became the theological swearing word of the hour" (Ward, *Religion and Society in England*, 18). David Bebbington agrees with Ward. Particularly, as Bebbington argues, Evangelicalism was a product of the Enlightenment. By placing eighteenth-century Evangelicalism and seventeenth-century Puritanism in contrast, Bebbington traces the former's source of influence to John Locke (1632-1704) and Isaac Newton (1643-1727) (see Bebbington, *Evangelicalism in Modern Britain: A History from the 1730s to the 1980s* [London; New York: Routledge1989], 50-60). Michael A.G. Haykin thus summarises the seventeenth-century approach to knowledge: "Seventeenth-century philosophical and scientific thought had been primarily concerned with general principles and the creation of metaphysical systems that would provide a unifying web for all fields of human knowledge" (Haykin, "Evangelicalism and the Enlightenment: A Reassessment," in *The Ardent of Evangelicalism: Exploring Historical Continuities*, edited by Michael A.G. Haykin, and Kenneth J. Stewart [Nashville, TN: B&H, 2008], 42). Furthermore, it seems that the eighteenth-century evangelicals—like many of their contemporary critics, such as David Hume (1711-1776)—adopted speculative metaphysics, while attacking the analytic metaphysics of their predecessors. Moreover, the eighteenth-century metaphysicians began to distinguish metaphysics from epistemology, ethics, and logic from a previous all-catch category of metaphysics. This trend of speculative metaphysics also paved the way for many late eighteenth-century Particular Baptists to adopt empiricism—at least in their approach to and view of the sacraments.

they are docile. And as you attend to the particular parts of Christianity,
it may be usefull to all your Students, (the best informed, as well as the most [10]
ignorant,) to refer to some Book, or some chapter in a Book, where the
subject then under review, is well treated. This would give them some
idea of Books, & might be useful afterwards.—
You will find it necessary to explain the nature of the different Systems which divide the religious world,
& to shew how their respective [15]
abettors reason upon them. This will very much instruct enquiring young
men & shorten their labour. We know not where
they may be placed, nor what
information
^ they may need. Besides the greater divisions, even the lesser parts may
require explanation. I have known a man in the ministry, a Calvinist,
who knew not what was meant by Supralapsarian & Sublapsarian.[12] [20]
Now without saying any thing about the importance of such distinctions,
(though every one must take a side) yet a preacher ought to know what
is meant by them, otherwise he may be in a situation where his ignorance
will be discreditable to him.
It will be needfull to point out the reasons of Dissent, however [25]
many became Ministers before they have known any thing of consequence
on this subject. And a Dissenting Minister who cannot state the ground of
his action with tolerable clearness, will cut a poor figure if he falls in the
way of a shroud Churchman.[13] For the same reason, some pains should be

---

[12] Supralapsarianism and sublapsarianism are two Reformed positions concerning the order of God's decrees. As Gregg Allison summarises: "The issue concerns whether logically, not temporally, God's decree to save people came before (Lat. *supra*) or after (*sub*) his decree to permit the fall (*lapsus*)" (Gregg R. Allison, *The Baker Compact Dictionary of Theological Terms* [Grand Rapids: Baker, 2016], 201, 204). Also see Herman Bavinck, *Reformed Dogmatics*, translated by John Vriend (Grand Rapids: Baker, 2004), 2:364–365; Curt D. Daiel, "Hyper-Calvinism and John Gill" (PhD diss., University of Edinburgh, 1983), 173–217; John Gill, *Truth Defended: Being an Answer to an Anonymous Pamphlet, intitled, Some Doctrines in the Superlapsarian Scheme impartially examined by the Word of God* (London: Aaron Ward, 1736). Though Kinghorn disagreed with the high Calvinists, it appears that Kinghorn took a Supralapsarian position, as he coined the three "principal pillars of Christianity," which were (1) "that the promise of Life was made (in Xt) before the World began Titus 1..2;" (2) "That by the deeds of the Law we cannot be justified;" and (3), "that our Justification is by Xt. thro Faith & that the nature of Justification by Faith & by the deeds of the Law are so opposite that it is in vain to attempt to mingle them together. Gal 3..11,12" (Joseph Kinghorn to David Kinghorn, January 31– February 1, 1791, D/KIN 2/1791 no. 651, [Angus Library and Archives, Regent's Park College, Oxford], 2).

[13] On Kinghorn's defence of the Dissenters, see [Joseph Kinghorn,] *Remarks on a "Country Clergyman's Attempt to Explain the Nature of the Visible Church, the Divine Commission of the Clergy, &c." Being a Defence of Dissenters in General, and of Baptists in Particular; on New Testament Principles* (Norwich: Simon Wilkin, 1829); Kinghorn, "Review of J.W. Cunningham's The Velvet Cushion, The Baptist Magazine, 1814," in Terry

[p. 5]
taken with respect to the most important principles of Church Government, [1]
to shew that the high church notion of Episcopacy has not a solid foundation. There has been bad reasoning on this subject on both sides. It will also be needfull to guard your Students against the System of the Scotch Dissenters, both Baptists and Independants [sic],
which we may call the Republicanism [5]
of Dissent;[14] A system that will in time prove itself to be in the wrong, but which during the trial may do a great deal of mischief.
It will be of great importance to impress the value of Truth on the minds of the young, & consequently to state the Evidence of what you feel to be of consequence, & to try to fix it in their hearts. I know the con [10]
tray way has some patrons, who say set before young persons both sides of a system, & without shewing your opinion of the value of either, let them choose for themselves. But whoever acts on this plan, either is indifferent to any thing, & thinks every sentiment may be equally useful, or he does not endeavour to do, what he might do for the cause of Truth. I believe it is [15]
known that very many of D<sup>r</sup>.. Doddridges' students imbibed opinions quite contrary to his;[15] & surely this was in part owing to an error in

---

Wolever, ed., *The Life and Works of Joseph Kinghorn* (Springfield, MO: Particular Baptist Press, 2010), 3: 229–238.

[14] Kinghorn seems to mean the church order of Scotch Baptists, not theological issues such as Sandemanianism or Archibald McLean's (1733–1812) rejection of the eternal sonship of Christ. By "Republicanism," Kinghorn probably meant the Wesleyan-Methodism-like connexionalism among the Scotch Baptists, in which "a strong leader was required to ensure the effective operation of their corporate activities" (Brian R. Talbot, *The Search for a Common Identity: The Origins of the Baptist Union of Scotland 1800–1870* [Milton Keyes, Buckinghamshire: Paternoster, 2003], 38). On the Scottish Independents, see Harry Escott, *A History of Scottish Congregationalism* (Glasgow: Congregational Union of Scotland, 1960). Also see Andrew T.N. Muirhead, *Reformation, Dissent and Diversity: The Story of Scotland's Churches, 1560–1960* (London; New York: Bloomsbury T&T Clark, 2015), 105–124.

[15] On Philip Doddridge (1702–1751), his pedagogy, and its effects, see Robert Strivens, "The Thought of Philip Doddridge in the Context of Early Eighteenth-Century Dissent" (PhD diss., University of Stirling, 2011), 42. Also see Philip Doddridge, *Sermons on the Religious Education of Children. Preached at Northampton* (London, 1732); Roger Thomas, "Philip Doddridge and Liberalism in Religion," in *Philip Doddridge, 1702-51: His Contribution to English Religion*, ed. Geoffrey F. Nuttall (London: Independent Press, 1951), 122–153; Alan P. F. Sell, *Philosophy, Dissent and Nonconformity* (Cambridge: Cambridge University Press, 2004); J. W. Ashley Smith, *The Birth of Modern Education: The Contribution of the Dissenting Academies, 1600–1800* (London: Independent Press, 1954), 138–143; A. Victor Murray, "Doddridge and Education," in *Philip Doddridge*, 102–121; Brad A. Thomas, "Teaching Against Tradition: Historical Preludes to Critical Pedagogy" (PhD diss., Texas A&M University, 2011). Also see Malcolm B. Yarnell, III, *John Locke's 'Letters of Gold': Universal Priesthood and the English Dissenting Theologians, 1688–1789* (Oxford: Regent's Park Col-

their education. Much as I esteem literature, & much as I have seen of the unpleasant effects of Ignorance in our ministers, I cannot think that any advantage arising from education, can be set against the evil of having our Churches supplied with ministers who deviate from what we believe is truth. If our preachers become cold & careless—mere moralizers in their sermons, or unitarians in their doctrine, it will soon ruin our denomination. Yet cases occur which require great tenderness & prudence. A young man may fall into serious perplexities on these points, & they may prove his trial. If he is carried away from the Doctrine of the Bible by his Speculations, his usefulness is destroyed: but if he overcomes his difficulties he is improved in mind, & sometimes ~~in usefulness~~ becomes an important character.[16]

[p. 6]
It will be right to form the students minds to a regard to scripture= criticism; but in doing this, you will endeavour to ~~erde~~ repress an inclination to appear <u>Learned</u>. The parade of Criticism seldom can do good;—often does hurt;—& in few instances consists with Christian Humility. A Book or a Sermon may evidently have been the result of much learned research, though it is not ostentatiously brought forward; & wherever we see this we always respect the author.[17]

---

lege, 2017); Russell E. Richey, "From Puritanism to Unitarianism in England: A Study in Candour," *Journal of the American Academy of Religion* 41.3 (1973): 371–385; Daniel E. White, *Early Romanticism and Religious Dissent* (Cambridge: Cambridge University Press, 2006); Tessa Whitehouse, ed., *Dissenting Education and the Legacy of John Jennings, c. 1720–c. 1729*, The Queen Mary Centre for Religion and Literature in English, http://www.qmulreligionandliterature.co.uk/online-publications/dissenting-education (accessed on November 17, 2019); Isabel Rivers, *The Defence of Truth through the Knowledge of Error: Philip Doddridge's Academy Lectures* (London: Dr Williams's Trust, 2003); Rivers, *Reason, Grace and Sentiment: A Study of the Language of Religion and Ethics in England, 1660-1780, Volume 2* (Cambridge: Cambridge University Press, 2000); Baiyu Andrew Song, "'When They Know Only or Chiefly Its Language, Not Its Spirit': Joseph Kinghorn (1766–1832) and Socinianism," *Puritan Reformed Journal* 12.2 (2020): 81–99. On Kinghorn's view of education, see Baiyu Andrew Song, "Joseph Kinghorn's (1766–1832) Educational Vision," *Pacific Journal of Theological Research* 15.1 (2020): 23–35.

[16] One example Kinghorn might have in mind was his classmate Samuel Pearce (1766–1799), who was perplexed by reading Joseph Priestley (1733–1804) and Daniel Whitby (1638–1736), and later was rescued from Socinianism and became a significant Baptist minister. See Andrew Fuller, *Memoirs of the Rev. Samuel Pearce*, The Complete Works of Andrew Fuller vol. 4, ed. Michael A.G. Haykin (Berlin; Boston: De Gruyter, 2017), 49–50, 123.

[17] In his response to the criticism of Charles Campbell (1791/1792–1887), vicar of All Saints, Weasenham, Norfolk, Kinghorn wrote: "learning is useful, and in some cases necessary, particularly in those controversies which are, in any measure, to be decided by literary criticism, is acknowledged by all, and by none more freely than by the 'uneducated and unlearned preachers of the word' [i.e. the dissenters). But

You will often find no small difficulty in teaching some to
express themselves clearly, and even in tolerable English. Many are brought
forward as preachers among us, whose habits were so far fixed before they [10]
began to speak ~~to others~~ on religious subjects publicly;—whose taste was
so initiated;—& whose ideas wore so contracted, that they always give the
Tutor a great deal of trouble. But these men are so important to our
Churches, that we should make many scarifies for their advantage.
They fill a number of pulpits which otherwise would be empty;— [15]
 greatly men
The real strength of a connexion ^ consists in those ^; they <u>labour</u> in the
 in obscurity
common cause ^, & they are often eminently useful.
With respect to the plan of conducting your pupils through a literary
course, you need no advice from me. When you come to teach Hebrew,
I hope your previous investigation of the nature of the Language, will lead you [20]
to teach it with the points. This I think has many advantages; and from
the little I know on the subject, it appears to me, that the popular Hutchinsonian plan, is the more abstract theory of a Modern.[18] One would hope that

---

does not the *Country Clergyman* know, that much more is necessary in numberless discussions than merely an ability to compare the 'English Bible with the Greek and Hebrew of the Original?' p. 15. Biblical criticism opens a large field of research. The state of the Text,—the force and proper meaning of unusual and peculiar expressions,—the sentiments and manner of thinking common among the people to whom the sacred writings were first addressed, are all subjects of consequence, and in some controversies much depends on their proper investigation. To make any proficiency in these enquiries, time, patient thinking, various reading, as well as respectable literature, are all needful; and those who in this line have distinguished themselves, have often shewn, that they did not hesitate to obtain information from any one who possessed it, without regarding the church to which he belonged, or even asking the question, *whether he had received the Holy Ghost, by the imposition of hands, or not*" ([Kinghorn,] *Remarks on a Country Clergyman's Attempt*, 25). Though Kinghorn highly approved the value of a learned ministry, he disagreed with the idea that only the educated could be ordained in the gospel ministry.

[18] John Hutchinson (1647–1737) was born at Spennithorne, Yorkshire and trained as a land steward. In 1694, Hutchinson was employed by Charles Seymour, the sixth Duke of Somerset. In 1700, Hutchinson was excited by John Woodward's (1665–1728)—the duke's physician—plan to reconcile the Old Testament with geology. Hutchinson then received funds from the duke to continue the project. As David S. Katz pointed out, "the Hutchinsonian scheme in its most active form was an amalgam of the original work of John Hutchinson and the reworded abstract of [Robert] Spearman [1703–1761] and [Julius] Bate [1711–1771]" (David S. Katz, "The Hutchinsonians and Hebraic Fundamentalism in Eighteenth-Century England," in *Sceptics, Millenarians and Jews*, edited by David S. Katz, and J.I. Israel [Leiden, the Netherlands: Brill, 1990], 238). The Hutchinsonian system began with "their faith in the Old Testament as the continuing revelation of God, and in the Hebrew language as the medium of its expression" (Katz, "The Hutchinsonians and Hebraic Fundamentalism in Eighteenth-Century England," 239). Thus, Hutchinson "sought to establish the primitive meanings of Hebrew roots in order to discover the true meaning of Scripture" (Marie-Louise Craig, "Hebrew-English Lexicons of the British Isles: From John Parkhurst (1762) to Benjamin Davies (1872)" [PhD

occasionally a Hebrew scholar might be raised up among us, who might arrive
the
at some distinction, & be able to meet ^ Jews on their own ground, but he could not
[25]
do this without some tolerable acquaintance with their system of pointing, whatever
he might think of its authority. But probably your opinion & mine coincide.
This however leads to a remark on Parkhursts Lexicon.[19] There are many excellent
things in it & much valuable criticism,
but I do not wish to see it become

[p. 7]
the popular Lexicon of our Students, because I am persuaded his theory of the
language [1]

---

diss., Charles Sturt University, 2014], 43). With the doctrine of Trinity, Hutchinson argued that the Jewish scholars had corrupted not only the Old Testament texts but also the Hebrew language, particularly by adding points. Thus, different from previous scholarship, Hutchinson sought to "identify one idea for each root and to rigorously apply that idea to all the words he considered were derived from that root" (Craig, "Hebrew-English Lexicons of the British Isles," 43). Also see David Paul Aikins Ney, "Scripture and Providence: The Hutchinsonian Quest to Save the Old Testament" (ThD diss., Wycliffe College and the University of Toronto, 2016); Derya Gurses, "The Hutchinsonian Defence of an Old Testament Trinitarian Christianity: The Controversy Over Elahim, 1735–1773," *History of European Ideas* 29 (2003): 393–409; Katz, "The Hutchinsonians and Hebraic Fundamentalism in Eighteenth-Century England," 237–255; John C. English, "John Hutchinson's Critique of Newtonian Heterodoxy," *Church History* 68.3 (1999): 581–597.

[19] John Parkhurst (1728–1797), *An Hebrew and English Lexicon. Without Points: In Which the Hebrew and Chaldee Words of the Old Testament are explained in their Leading and Derived Senses, the Derivative Words are ranged under their respective Primitives, and the Meanings assigned to each Authorised by References to Passages of Scripture. To this Work is prefixed a Methodical Hebrew Grammar, Without Points; Adapted to the Use of Learners, and of those who have not the Benefit of a Master: Also, the Hebrew Grammar, at One View* (London: W. Faden, 1762). Parkhurst was born to John Parkhurst at Catesby Priory, near Daventry. He attended Clare Hall, Cambridge, where he obtained the degrees of B.A. (1748) and M.A. (1752) and was elected Fellow and sixth Wrangler in 1748. Since his early days, Parkhurst became a follower of John Hutchinson, particularly following his principles of biblical exegesis. Parkhurst's Hebrew Lexicon went through four editions and several reprinting, and it was regarded as an extraordinary Hebrew dictionary. On Parkhurst, see Anonymous, "A Brief Sketch of the Life of the Late Rev. John Parkhurst, A.M.," in John Parkhurst, *An Hebrew and English Lexicon*, 5th ed. (London, 1807), iii–vii; Craig, "Hebrew-English Lexicons of the British Isles;" Anonymous, *The Rugby Register, from the Year 1675* (Rugby: Crossley and Billington, 1853), 42; Francis Whellan, *History, Topography, and Directory of Northamptonshire*, 2nd ed. (London: Whittaker and Co., 1874), 392.

In a letter to his father, Joseph Kinghorn recommended Parkhurst's Lexicon. In addition, Kinghorn noted that Parkhurst's is "a usefull Book but a book not to be implicitly relied on" (Joseph Kinghorn to David Kinghorn, June 11, 1799, D/KIN 2/1799 no. 985, Kinghorn Papers [Angus Library and Archives, Regent's Park College, Oxford], 2).

is in many places wrong.[20]
Your enquire about Books on the office of a Tutor. I know none on
that subject expressly. The Biography of such men as have been Tutors, will
furnish your wish the best information on that subject; as it will shew how [5]
different men of talent thought and acted, whereas a Book would only shew
you one man's plan. Doddridges's Life will afford many useful hints.[21]
I lately read a pamphlet by the late M$^r$. Newton of S$^t$.. Mary's Woolnoth
first published in 1784,[22] and now in the 9$^{th}$.. vol of the 12$^{mo}$. Edinburgh ed. of
his Works,[23] in which are some good things, as far as it goes; It is a Utopian
scene, but [10]
was evidently a cover, that under it he might say what he pleased
But I think, & probably you think, that it is high time for me to conclude

May God in his Mercy bless you, & crown your labours with abundant success.
I shall be glad to hear from you at any time. The pamphlet you mention

---

[20] Like Hutchinson, Parkhurst also believed in the divine origin of the Hebrew language, and it is "the common mother of … all other languages" (Parkhurst, *Hebrew and English Lexicon*, b2). Furthermore, by adopting a primitive view, Parkhurst argued that "each Hebrew root has but one leading idea or meaning, taken from nature by our senses or feelings, which runs through all the branches and deflections of it, however numerous or diversified" (Parkhurst, *Hebrew and English Lexicon* [London, 1762], iii). Thus, in every entry, Parkhurst aimed to "show how the primitive idea of the root was worked out through all the derivatives of that same root. He did not recognize the possibility of homonymy. He believed that words with the same permanent radicals belonged to the same root" (Craig, "Hebrew-English Lexicons of the British Isles," 52). By rejecting Jewish scholarship, Parkhurst worked explicitly to make a case for the doctrine of Trinity in the Old Testament, which for him, was intentionally corrupted by the Jews through manipulating and corrupting words and grammar.

[21] Kinghorn might refer to Job Orton's *Memoirs of the Life, Character and Writings of the Late Reverend Philip Doddridge, D.D. of Northampton* (Salop, 1766).

[22] John Newton (1725–1807), *A Plan of Academical Preparation for the Ministry, in a Letter to a Friend*, 2nd ed. (n.p., 1784). This letter was first written on May 14, 1782, and was published in the same year. In this 53-page letter, Newton proposed a theological academy in Utopia. Newton's three maxims or educational principles are: "that none but He who made the World can make a Minister of the Gospel;" "That the Holy scriptures are both comprehensively and exclusively, the grand treasury of all that knowledge which is requisite and sufficient, to make the Minister, the Man of God, thoroughly furnished for every branch of his office;" and "That the true Gospel Minister who possesses these secondary advantages, though he may know the same things, and acquire his knowledge by the like methods, as other scholars do, yet he must know and possess them in a manner peculiar to himself" (Newton, *Plan of Academical Preparation for the Ministry*, 2–4). Under these principles, Newton provided advice on the location, the tutor, the pupils, and the course of education at his imagined academy.

[23] It appears that Kinghorn owned a set of John Newton's works, which was published at Edinburgh in 1809. This set contains 11 volumes with a biography written by Richard Cecil (1748–1810). See [Simon Wilkin, ed.,] *Catalogue of the Entire Library of the Late Rev. Joseph Kinghorn, of Norwich* (Norwich: Wilkin and Fletcher, 1833), 32.

I have never rec^d..²⁴ I conclude sincerely yours in the Gospel [15]

Norwich May 13, 1811                                    Jos.. Kinghorn

---

²⁴ Since Newman's letter was not preserved, it is unclear to which pamphlet Kinghorn was referring. Nevertheless, it is quite possible that this pamphlet was Andrew Fuller's *Strictures on Sandemanianism, in Twelve Letters to a Friend* (Nottingham: C. Sutton, 1810), as Newman mentioned earlier in his diary that he read Fuller's pamphlet on February 9, 1811 (William Newman's Diary, D/NEW1/1808–1818, volume 1 [Angus Library and Archive, Regent's Park College, Oxford]).

# Book reviews

Crawford Gribben, and Graeme Murdock, eds., *Cultures of Calvinism in Early Modern Europe* (New York, NY: Oxford University Press, 2019), x + 254 pages.

By reading the title of this volume, readers are introduced to a number of questions. For one, what is "Calvinism"? This issue is raised in the introduction, where the editors, Crawford Gribben and Graeme Murdock, describe "early modern Calvinism" as "something of a moving target" (p. 5). The opening chapter "Describing Calvinism" by Todd Rester also addresses this issue and concludes that "the use of the term 'Calvinism' as an early modern descriptor must be contextualized and qualified, given that the Reformed generally rejected the term" (p. 35). Instead of neatly setting up the work with a clearly defined understanding of "Calvinism," the introduction and the opening chapter correctly display the difficulty and the debates surrounding this term.

From there, the readers then need to deal with the question of "culture" and the selective nature by which authors will have to choose concerning the aspect of culture they want to write about. Readers also must realize the selective nature of what part of the "early modern" period that is going to be addressed, and furthermore, what location of "Europe." These issues are also raised in the introduction, as the editors admit that the chapters do not cover all the locations across Europe, nor are they "confined by clear chronological limits" (p. 7). Taken together, the title of the volume presents the reader with an uncertainty of what "culture" of "Calvinism" they are going to read about, and from what span of the "early modern" period and from what location in "Europe" that this "culture" comes from.

With this broad range of possibilities, one must come to the work with an open mind of what may be addressed. The book presents a collection of chapters divided into three parts—the first on "cultures of the Word," the second on "visual and performing cultures," and the third on "cultures of behavior." Each section includes different chapters on a variety of topics—from education (chapter 3 by D.G. Hart), philosophy (chapter 4 by Paul Helm), theatre (chapter 6 by Freya Sierhuis and Adrian Streete), and war (chapter 9 by Christine Kooi)—each written by different authors, representing a range of disciplines. Each chapter is in some way connected to the culture of "Calvinism" or the Reformed tradition and span greatly in the geography and time periods that they focus on. Some chapters deal with several locations across different centuries; others are more focused in time and location. Throughout, the volume seems unsure with what exactly to do with the term "Calvinism" and it is often seemingly used synonymously with the Reformed tradition. This of course raises the question of who gets to define who is and is not "Reformed." Regardless of this uncertainty, as a whole, the volume provides the readers with much variety in terms of topics, methods, and fields of study.

Such variety leads to both benefits and weaknesses. The benefits are found in reading about areas that one will likely not be familiar with. Based on the variety of topics, locations, and time periods, it is quite likely that one will subsequently learn something new from the reading. Moreover, this volume helps to show the breadth of the Reformed tradition by showing how it was received, applied, and developed in a variety of places in different time periods. The weakness of such a volume, however, is that it cannot be all things to all people. One may be disappointed to not find discussions on certain places in Europe, or to not see a certain aspect of culture written on, or to see that a group or author one may identify as being within the "Calvinist" tradition is not discussed at length.

With the latter in mind, the readers of this journal may be disappointed to find little on the Baptists. Indeed, the question of Baptists and the Reformed tradition is a debated one (see Matthew C. Bingham, Chris Caughey, R. Scott Clark, Crawford Gribben, and D.G. Hart, *On Being Reformed: Debates over a Theological Identity* [Cham, Switzerland: Palgrave Pivot, 2018]), but at the least one would hope to see the Particular Baptists connected to certain understandings of "Calvinism." Yet the Baptists are given scant attention, with only brief and passing references. Although John Bunyan is mentioned in a few different places, no extended discussion is given to his works; at the least, one would expect a further discussion of *Pilgrim's Progress* in the chapter on "Calvinism and Literature" by Mark Sweetnam. But as it is, Baptists are solely peripheral and only mentioned in passing.

A person looking for an extended discussion on Baptists should thus not look to this collection. However, for those broadly interested in the influence of "Calvinism" on a variety of topics in the early modern period, it will be an interesting read. As is to be expected in a collected volume, some chapters are stronger than others, and some are more general and others more focused. But overall, this is a volume accessible to a variety of readers with a range of interests. It is a welcome addition to the topic of the influence of "Calvinism" on culture and opens the door to further studies in the future.

Jonathan N. Cleland
PhD cand., Knox College, University of Toronto
Toronto, Ontario, Canada

---

Kyle C. Strobel, Adriaan C. Neele, and Kenneth P. Minkema, eds., *Jonathan Edwards: Spiritual Writings*, Classics of Western Spirituality (Mahwah, NJ: Paulist Press, 2019), 440 pages.

Jonathan Edwards is America's foremost theologian is a rule-of-thumb for historians that the passage of time has only further confirmed. The renaissance of Edwardsean scholarship, prompted by the publication of Perry Miller's 1949 biography of the New England divine, and the completion of a half-century's scholarly labors on the critical edition of Edwards' corpus by Yale University Press, exposure to his writings—with the exception of academic and confessionally Calvinist circles in Britain and North America—has been limited. There is no evidence, for example, that the eminent Swiss theologian Karl Barth (1886–1968), who possessed a rich knowledge of the Reformed tradition, ever read Edwards.

Paulist Press' release of an edited selection of *Spiritual Writings* in the coveted *Classics of Western Spirituality* increases the likelihood that a future theologian of Barth's stature will be familiar with Edwards. As for a wider audience, the rapid growth of Christianity in the global south where revivals akin to that of Northampton in the 1730's and 40's are a present reality, Edwards theological assessments will be of immense value.

This book provides a necessary but not overwhelming introduction to the author, his context, and the selected writings. In the prelude, Adriaan Neele places Edwards in the broader scholastic tradition in which theology constituted a "mixed discipline," consisting of theory and praxis, though it leaned towards the latter (p. 2). The book is divided into five sections: (1) the general contours of Edwards' spirituality, (2) affections, (3) beauty, (4) means of grace, and (5) the internal and external means of grace. The largest number of pages are devoted to sections two and five.

Part I features selections familiar to readers of Edwards, including his "Resolutions" (pp. 55–62), *Faithful Narrative* (pp. 77–84), and *Diary of David Brainerd* (pp. 85–88). The editors are keen to juxtapose earlier writings with Edwards' mature thought, contrasting the zealous rigor of the young pastor with the seasoned opinions that came with experience and reflection.

In Part II, an excerpt from *Religious Affections*, is 35 pages, forming—justifiability—the longest selection from a single work in the volume. Included in "Affections," are the ecstatic experiences of Sarah Edwards that occurred in 1742, and which were assiduously documented by her husband. Such accounts remind readers that the spiritual awakenings in Edwards' day defy neat or facile assessment. For example, a 1748 sermon, *Extraordinary Gifts of the Spirit are Inferior to Graces of the Spirit* (pp. 390–399) exemplifies a classic Reformed exposition of cessationism. Edwards evidently felt no conflict existed between Sarah's "Narrative" and a confidence that miraculous gifts were limited to Apostolic times.

Aesthetics constitute the third portion of the book, featuring some of Edwards most illuminating reflections on beauty. The editors draw memorable and penetrating pastoral observations from several sermons. In "Heaven is a World of Love," he writes, "the saints shall know that God loves them, and they shall not doubt the greatness of his love; and they shall have no doubt of the love of all their heavenly inhabitants" (p. 245). Such selections serve to remind readers that "Sinners in the Hands of an Angry God" is exceptional rather than normative in the preaching ministry of Edwards.

The fourth part provides a window into the tension between Edwards' unwavering commitment to the sovereignty of God, and the duty Christians have to pursue holiness. He explains the nature and effects of means of grace in "Miscellanies" no. 539, which reads, "the means of grace have no influence to work grace, but only give such notions to our minds, and so disposed, as to give opportunity to grace to act, when God shall infuse it" (p. 278). Wary of any notion of *opere ex operato*, Edwards nevertheless finds a consistent pattern that, if it cannot be called causation proper, is quite proximate to cause and effect.

The fifth and final part to *Spiritual Writings* features Edwards' understanding of the internal and external work of grace. Considering the sermon, *A Spiritual Understanding of Divine Things Denied to the Unregenerate* (pp. 320–345) was preached when Edwards was only 20 years-old, predating Whitefield's first preaching tour to America by nearly two decades, is remarkable. His insistence on the need for spiritual illumination, and his exhortation that hearers not be prejudiced against such illumination was atypical for the time, a detail modern readers of Edwards can miss.

Eighteenth-century prose presents challenges to unaccustomed readers, and Edwards can be particularly dense. Patient and careful engagement with the material will, however, prove a worthwhile investment.

The late Sydney Ahlstrom noted that Jonathan Edwards' theological vision was not embraced by subsequent generations of American Congregationalists. Even his most gifted intellectual disciples, Joseph Bellamy and Samuel Hopkins, broke with their teacher at significant junctures, thereby placing these theologians in a school of their own—the New Divinity. The world has changed dramatically since Edwards' death in 1758, yet his writings have not aged in the way opponents, and even his contemporary admirers feared. Scores have read *Religious Affections* and *The Diary of David Brainerd*. Those familiar with Bellamy and Hopkins are a scholarly niche.

The search for Edwardian heirs is thus ongoing, and the present volume will assure wider dissemination of his ideas. The potential for twenty-first century readers to appropriate Edwards in fruitful and significant ways is promising.

Ryan Rindels
Gateway Seminary of Southern Baptist Convention, Ontario, CA
Pastor, First Baptist Church of Sonoma, CA

---

Sean McGever, *Born Again: The Evangelical Theology of Conversion in John Wesley and George Whitefield*. Studies in Historical and Systematic Theology (Bellingham, WA: Lexham Press, 2020), x + 249 pages.

No discussion of eighteenth-century evangelicalism is complete without consideration of the life and thought of John Wesley and George Whitefield. While known for their disagreements over the areas of Arminianism and Calvinism, comparisons of other aspects of their theology are less prominent. One such aspect is looked at in this study, where, McGever argues, despite their differing views on certain topics, their theologies of conversion share many similarities. These similarities are based on the thesis that "Wesley and Whitefield's theologies of conversion are best understood in terms of inaugurated teleology with an emphasis on the *telos* of salvation rather than the *arché* of salvation" (p. 13). Put simply, both Wesley and Whitefield agree that conversion is not an end of itself, but is meant to begin a process of salvation that leads to sanctification in the life of the individual. This thesis is argued for throughout the book not simply as an exercise in historical theology for interest's sake, but for the sake of offering "renewed reflection and response to the issues raised by evangelical theologians on the topic of conversion" (p. 4). In a time where the evangelical world may focus solely at the beginning of conversion, McGever, through the work of Whitefield and Wesley, challenges people to understand conversion as having a *telos* that directs people toward a holistic Christian life.

This book is divided into seven chapters. The first chapter introduces the book, and chapters two through five deal with Wesley and then Whitefield's view of conversion. The sixth chapter compares Wesley and Whitefield's theology of conversion, and the seventh chapter uses their historical-theological views to challenge modern characterizations of conversion. The book closes with a bibliography and subject and scripture indexes.

The similarities shared between Wesley and Whitefield are structured around nine statements. The first seven are on conversion; conversion (1) "is initiated and sustained by grace," (2) "is the experiential correlate to salvation," (3) "is a turning *from* self and *to* Christ," (4) "is foreshadowed by a deep sense of sinfulness," (5) "arrives by faith in an instant," (6) "is instantaneous but is not always recognizable on behalf of the convert," and (7) "is marked by ongoing good works." The final two statements are (8) "baptism marks one's entrance to the church but is not chronologically tied to conversion," and (9) "assurance of salvation is available but not required for a genuine convert" (p. 2). Although these statements show areas of agreement, McGever also points out "election, predestination, irresistible grace, imputation, perseverance, and Christian perfection" as areas of disagreement between the two theologians (p. 2).

The historical-theological work on Wesley and Whitefield's thought shows evidence of careful scholarship. McGever describes the thought of both theologians within the context of their historical intellectual *milieu*. McGever does not shy away from the reality of development in the theologians' careers, as he traces "four distinct transitions" in Wesley's view of assurance and conversion (p. 77), and he also avoids the tendency to discredit potentially difficult views for contemporary readers, as is evidenced in his nuanced presentation of Whitefield's view of baptismal regeneration. While there is a danger for theological retrieval to oversimplify historical theology for the sake of present-day relevance, McGever is careful to provide the historical research of Wesley and Whitefield first before then offering their thought as a corrective for evangelicals today.

Concerning readership, the book is written and structured in a way that is clear and accessible for the pastor and scholar alike. The historical content offers an important contribution to the studies of Wesley and Whitefield, and the theological content offers challenge and correction to contemporary

Christians and pastors. With its attractive cover and binding along with its reasonable price, this volume is a welcome study for a variety of readers.

Jonathan N. Cleland<br>
PhD cand., Knox College, University of Toronto<br>
Toronto, Ontario, Canada

---

Eric C. Smith, *Oliver Hart and the Rise of Baptist America* (New York, NY: Oxford University Press, 2020), 337 pages.

For Baptists in America the long eighteenth century proved to be nothing short of transformative—both in terms of sheer growth as well as denominational maturation. In *Oliver Hart and the Rise of Baptist America*, Eric C. Smith traces the story of Baptist development in America throughout this period by looking to one of the foremost proponents of the "Baptist interest," Oliver Hart. The longtime pastor of First Baptist Church of Charleston, Oliver Hart, has long been regarded as one of the most influential leaders who steered Baptist development in the American South. According to Smith, Hart's contribution "extended far beyond the Baptist South" as he sought to unite all Baptists on the continent (p. 5). The Charleston pastor not only worked to overcome geographical challenges to Baptist unity, but also proved instrumental in bringing together Separate and Regular Baptists, creating a denominational infrastructure, gaining respectability, securing religious liberty, and encouraging revival.

Smith begins his saga of Hart's life and ministry by situating the Charleston preacher within his family context. His grandfather was a Quaker turned Baptist in colonial Pennsylvania. Thus, Hart was steeped in the tradition of the Pennepek Baptist Church and the Philadelphia Association from an early age. As Smith details, however, Hart would experience conversion in 1740 not through the ordinary ministry of the colonial Particular Baptists, but rather through the extraordinary revivals associated with the Great Awakening. Within Hart a synthesis emerged between the traditional theology and practice of his Calvinistic Baptist forebearers and the evangelical emphasis on conversion and revival associated with the awakening.

Having been affirmed in his fitness for ministry, the Pennsylvania native accepted a call to pastor a fledgling congregation in the South, Charleston Baptist Church. With little Baptistic influence in that area at the time, Hart "purposed to establish a strategic beachhead for Baptist life in the South, importing the model of moderate revivalism and Baptist denominal order he had experienced in the Philadelphia Association" (p. 80). Under his labor and leadership, the Charleston Baptist Church grew in size and influence. Smith demonstrates that Hart did not limit his efforts to the local church but initiated the "first denomination meeting among Baptist churches of the South" when he led in the formation of the Charleston Association in 1751 (p. 105). Having solidified his church and established an association, Hart's prayers for an awakening were answered in 1754 when revival broke out in Charleston. As seasons of revival swept through the colonies during the mid-eighteenth century, Hart became known for his leadership and support of the evangelical awakening.

When revival gave way to the American Revolution, Hart never wavered in his support for independence. The Charleston pastor was asked to engage in a tour through the backcountry of his state in order to convince loyalists to support the cause of the patriots, serving as proof of his notoriety. Because of his vocal support of the revolutionary cause, Hart was forced to flee Charleston upon its capture in 1780. He returned to his native Philadelphia area, where he was asked to fill the pulpit of the Hopewell Baptist Church of New Jersey. Following the war, Hart made the difficult decision to remain at Hopewell, where he continued to promote the Baptist cause. While he never returned to Charleston, Smith sums up Hart's influence when he writes, "the center of gravity for Baptist America was beginning to shift from North to South, due in no small part to Hart's own labors in Charleston" (pp. 277–278). Near the end of 1795, the aging Hart breathed his last. While he had accomplished much for Baptists within his lifetime, Smith demonstrates that Hart's vision for widespread Baptist cooperation would come to be fulfilled in the formation of the Triennial Convention, the Southern Baptist Convention, and The Southern Baptist Theological Seminary.

In *Oliver Hart and the Rise of Baptist America* Smith has written an engaging biography of an influential Baptist leader, as well as a gripping narrative of the rise of a denomination within the eighteenth century American religious landscape. Each chapter situates a portion of Hart's life within the surrounding context in order to introduce readers to the larger religious currents within which American Baptists found themselves. For example, in chapter two, which focuses on Hart's conversion, Smith weaves Hart's story within the larger context of the Great Awakening. Thus, readers are left not only with an engaging personal narrative but also with a helpful survey of the period in view.

Smith's well researched and lucidly written work fills a major lacuna in Baptist studies by providing a focused history of eighteenth-century American Baptist development. Furthermore, by focusing on the life and ministry of Oliver Hart and his promotion of the "Baptist interest," Smith tells a multi-faceted story that captures both the denominational history as well as the realities of everyday existence as lived by one leading exponent. *Oliver Hart and the Rise of Baptist America* deserves a wide reading among historians of the period as well as those who maintain some affinity with the denomination "covered in Hart's fingerprints" (p. 314).

Dustin Bruce<br>
Boyce College, Louisville, KY<br>
Dean, and Assistant Professor of Christian Theology and Church History

---

Kevin DeYoung, *The Religious Formation of John Witherspoon: Calvinism, Evangelicalism, and the Scottish Enlightenment*. Routledge Studies in Evangelicalism (New York, NY: Routledge, 2020), x + 211 pages.

John Witherspoon, the eighteenth-century Scottish pastor and subsequent a founding father of the United States, is known more for having been the New Jersey delegate who signed the American Constitution than for his ministry in his native Scotland. In this book, Kevin DeYoung reverses this emphasis by detailing Witherspoon's pastoral work, as well as by exploring his theology in light of his ministry. DeYoung asserts that Witherspoon's theological thought may not fully be "understood until we see him not only *engaged* with the Scottish Enlightenment, but also *firmly grounded* in the Reformed tradition of High to Late Orthodoxy, *embedded* in the transatlantic evangelical awakenings of the eighteenth century, and *frustrated* by the state of religion in the Scottish Kirk" (p. 4). In the first four chapters, DeYoung expounds upon each of these ideas, while in the fifth chapter he argues that Witherspoon's theology and ministry in Scotland was more consistent with his thought and work in America than has been previously thought.

The connections drawn by DeYoung between the afore-mentioned considerations are apt. He offers persuasive and cogent historical scholarship which display Witherspoon clearly as a pastor knowledgeable of his own tradition—a man who was firmly situated within the Reformed and evangelical camps. Despite such encampment, however, Witherspoon as a theologian still left much to be desired. His theological thought is largely predictable, as DeYoung presents him as often "sticking closely to the Westminster Confession of Faith and the traditional side of Reformed orthodoxy" (p. 49). In this way Witherspoon can clearly be seen as one who continued in the Reformed tradition yet did not contribute to any significant theological innovations within it. While this is acceptable for the character of a pastor, this relegates a study of his theology as less interesting. Even with this criticism, this book is written in a clear and engaging manner and is a fine example of careful scholarship of a key figure in American history. Thus, this work is likely to find its place primarily on the bookshelf of two types of readers—among those involved in Witherspoon studies, and those interested in the reception of the evangelical and Reformed tradition in the eighteenth century.

Jonathan N. Cleland
PhD cand., Knox College, University of Toronto
Toronto, Ontario, Canada

# CENTER *for* BAPTIST STUDIES
*at* THE SOUTHERN BAPTIST THEOLOGICAL SEMINARY

The Andrew Fuller Center for Baptist Studies, located at The Southern Baptist Theological Seminary in Louisville, Kentucky, seeks to promote the study of Baptist history as well as theological reflection on the contemporary significance of that history. The center is named in honor of Andrew Fuller (1754–1815), the late eighteenth- and early nineteenth- century English Baptist pastor and theologian, who played a key role in opposing aberrant thought in his day as well as being instrumental in the founding and early years of the Baptist Missionary Society. Fuller was a close friend and theological mentor of William Carey, one of the pioneers of that society.

The Andrew Fuller Center holds an annual two-day conference in September that examines various aspects of Baptist history and thought. It also supports the publication of the critical edition of the Works of Andrew Fuller, and from time to time, other works in Baptist history. The Center seeks to play a role in the mentoring of junior scholars interested in studying Baptist history.

andrewfullercenter.org

## The Andrew Fuller Works Project

It is with deep gratitude to God that The Andrew Fuller Center for Baptist Studies announces that the publishing house of Walter de Gruyter, with head offices in Berlin and Boston, has committed itself to the publication of a modern critical edition of the entire corpus of Andrew Fuller's published and unpublished works. Walter de Gruyter has been synonymous with high-quality, landmark publications in both the humanities and sciences for more than 260 years. The preparation of a critical edition of Fuller's works, part of the work of the Andrew Fuller Center, was first envisioned in 2004. It is expected that this edition this edition will comprise seventeen volumes.

## The importance of the project

The controlling objective of The Works of Andrew Fuller Project is to preserve and accurately transmit the text of Fuller's writings. The editors are committed to the finest scholarly standards for textual transcription, editing, and annotation. Transmitting these texts is a vital task since Fuller's writings, not only for their volume, extent, and scope, but for their enduring importance, are major documents in both the Baptist story and the larger history of British Dissent.

From a merely human perspective, if Fuller's theological works had not been written, William Carey would not have gone to India. Fuller's theology was the mainspring behind the formation and early development of the Baptist Missionary Society, the first foreign missionary society created by the Evangelical Revival of the last half of the eighteenth century and the missionary society under whose auspices Carey went to India. Very soon, other missionary societies were established, and a new era in missions had begun as the Christian faith was increasingly spread outside of the West, to the regions of Africa and Asia. Carey was most visible at the fountainhead of this movement. Fuller, though not so visible, was utterly vital to its genesis.

andrewfullercenter.org/the-andrew-fuller-works-project

H&E Publishing is a Canadian evangelical publishing company located out of Peterborough, Ontario. We exist to provide Christ-exalting, Gospel-centred, and Bible-saturated content aimed to show God to be as glorious and worthy as He truly is.

hesedandemet.com

www.ingramcontent.com/pod-product-compliance
Lightning Source LLC
Chambersburg PA
CBHW030040100526
44590CB00011B/273